The History, Practice, and Future of
Cheating Death

The History, Practice, and Future of Cheating Death

Written by: Austin Mardon, Thomas Banks, Madeline Langier, Rob Mcweeny, Jonathan Wiebe & Catherine Mardon

Edited by: Alyssa Kulchisky

Designed by: Josh Kramer

Published by Golden Meteorite Press
2021

The History, Practice, and Future of Cheating Death
Copyright © 2021 by Austin Mardon
All rights reserved.

This book or any portion thereof may not be reproduced or used in any manner whatsoever without the express written permission of the publisher except for the use of brief quotations in a review.

The authors of this book are not healthcare professionals. The content of this book should not be interpreted as prescribing or recommending any particular medical treatments. Always consult your healthcare practitioner to manage your health.

First Printing: 2021

ISBN: 978-1-77369-603-4

Golden Meteorite Press
103 11919 82 St NW
Edmonton, AB T5B 2W3
www.goldenmeteoritepress.com
aamardon@yahoo.ca
Alberta, Canada

Table of Contents

Chapter 1: The Search for Eternal Youth 1
Chapter 2: Global Perspectives on Ageing, Youth & Vitality ... 13
Chapter 3: Social Impacts of Anti-Ageing 33
Chapter 4: Socioeconomic Factors 45
Chapter 5: Current Anti-Ageing Medicine and Technology ... 53
Chapter 6: The Future of Anti-Ageing Medicine
and Technology 67
Chapter 7: Economic Benefits to Anti-Ageing
and Healthspan Extension 89
Chapter 8: Ethical Issues With Eternal Youth 103
Chapter 9: A Blessing Or A Curse? 119
Chapter 10: Alternative Routes To Immortality 139
References 153

Chapter I
The Search for Eternal Youth

"Eternal youth is impossible. Even if there is no other obstacle, introspection would make it impossible."

- Franz Kafka

Introduction

Science and spirituality collide in the desire for eternal youth. Legends of eternal youth have survived for thousands of years and have contributed to the modern understanding of longevity and eternal youth. The following chapter describes various legends and anti-ageing practices throughout history. The road to eternal youth is littered with strange and fascinating methods. While many were dangerous or ineffective they paved the way for the search for extended life and preserved youth.

Increased longevity, a longer life, is, in essence, to defy nature by increasing the human lifespan past what may be considered natural. Hence, increased longevity or the ability to acquire eternal life has long been associated with the divine. Today, modern science has begun to provide a taste of what only the Gods have had, eternal life. Advancements in technology, medicine and overall human intelligence have bestowed the human race with the gift of a bit more time on earth. Currently, cryogenic freezing and stem cell research are at the forefront of cosmetic anti-ageing and longevity treatments affecting the human lifespan. Further, caloric reduction and research to slow or stop cell decay are widely considered the most effective and innovative methods to accomplish increased longevity. For more information on current anti-ageing and longevity technologies turn to chapter 5. Before modern technology, cryogenic freezing for cosmetic anti-ageing was used to various ends (although not for freezing the body for a century to unfreeze when science has found a cure for ageing). Rather, freezing as an anti-ageing treatment targets the outer layer of the skin to impact deep layers of collagen and is known as cryotherapy. Medical professionals have been using cryotherapy for nearly 100 years to treat common skin conditions (Andrew, 2004). Specifically, cryotherapy is used to treat benign skin conditions and is considered cryosurgery by modern medicine. In cryosurgery, liquid nitrogen is applied to the skin using a cotton tip or a liquid nitrogen spray (Andrew, 2004). Frigid temperatures are used to freeze off any abnormal skin tissue, and research has found it may be effective in treating acute injuries (Hubbard et al., 2004).

Further, cryosurgery helps treat skin infections such as warts and is incredibly useful in treating sun-damaged skin and related skin issues (Andrew, 2014). Cryogenic therapy has made its way to the mainstream consumer market and is used as a tool to zap away ageing and fat cells to maintain the appearance of youth and virility. However, cryotherapy research is not necessarily marketed in the medical field as an anti-ageing treatment. While it is used cosmetically to treat superficial elements of skincare cryogenic therapies, it assists in longevity because it increases the quality of life. Therefore cryotherapy is a unique tool with the potential to contribute to the well-being and superficial elements of longevity.

Before modern science, various metaphysical elements were speculated on to address ageing. The earliest known record mentioning the search for eternal life is found in the ancient

Mesopotamian poem about the King and demigod, Gilgamesh. An English archaeologist and explorer, Austen Henry Layard, discovered the Epic of Gilgamesh in 1849 CE. The epic, a long poem describing the various perilous adventures undertaken by the heroes of days long past, dates back to the Mesopotamian era, which roughly spanned from 500 BCE and 400 CE. Layard discovered the epic on twelve stone tablets in the ruins of the ancient library Ashurbanipal in the Sumerian language, although it was later translated into Akkadian, the native tongue of the Mesopotamian empire (Mark, 2021). Most notable is that the epic features Gilgamesh and his human struggles against death, loss and the seemingly meaningless human existence. While the epic is widely known as a legend containing many mystical elements, many scholars believe Gilgamesh to be a real ancient king who ruled the city of Uruk 100 years before the creation of the stone tablets.

In the epic, Enkidu, a wild man tamed by a temple concubine, is brought to the city of Uruk. Enkidu challenges Gilgameshto a battle and is overcome, after which the two warriors pledge themselves to each other in a pact of eternal friendship. Further, Gilgamesh's mother adopts Enkidu as her own. The pair share an intimate bond. Eventually Enkidu dies, and Gilgamesh becomes lost, leading him to search for the cure to death. In his despair, Gilgamesh ventures to the Land of Night and the Waters of Death, where he finds the ancient man Utanapishtim, the only human being to survive the Great Flood who was afterwards granted immortality (Mark, 2021). Utanapishtim tells Gilgamesh the story of how he was warned by the god Ea of the coming deluge, followed his command to build an ark, place assorted animals inside, and save himself and his family from death and humanity from extinction. He then tells Gilgamesh that eternal life will be granted if the great King can stay awake for the next six days; he is unable to. In a second attempt for the gift of eternal youth, Gilgamesh found and aimed to retrieve a magic plant that would make one young again. According to the legend, a snake ate the plant while Gilgamesh slept. Simply, the magic plant gave the snake its ability to rejuvenate. Having failed to win immortality, Gilgamesh is brought back to Uruk by the ferryman Urshanabi where, once home, he writes down his great adventure (Mark, 2021). According to the historian D. Brendan Nagle, the poem deals with human problems such as sickness, death, fame, and unattainable desires. Furthermore, the epic could be considered a metaphor for Mesopotamia's own heroic struggle to resist decay and leave a name for itself among the peoples of earth (Mark, 2021). Regardless of the assumptions that might be made about the meaning of the story, ultimately Gilgamesh fails his epic mission to attain eternal life.

While the Epic of Gilgamesh encapsulates the search for longevity to evade death, others seek to avoid ageing. The search for eternal life is not the same as the desire for eternal youth in that eternal life includes the functioning of the body for eternity whereas ageing is a superficial element typically connected to what we can see. The Byzantine Empress Zoe Porphyrogenita effectively represents many peoples' continuous struggle for eternal youth rather than the desire for eternal life. Among the living from 978 to 1050 and a beautiful empress, Empress Zoe Porphyrogenita was blonde, with bright white smooth skin well into her sixties. Moreover, she was described as child-like, sharing features with a very young girl (Panas et al., 2012). Historians describe the Empress as entirely committed to formulating cosmetic extracts. She installed a laboratory in her private quarters in the palace where she spent most of her time manufacturing drugs and perfumes (Panas et al., 2012). Various sources suggest she also spent time making drugs and poisons, which she may have been used to poison each of her husbands. With this in mind, she married three times, at the ages of fifty, fifty-six, and sixty-four; the third time the bridegroom was roughly twenty years old. According to the eyewitness of those times, Byzantine historian and courtier Michael Psellos (1018 - c. 1082 CE), Empress Zoe had blonde hair into old age. Further, Psellos writes: "although she had already passed her seventieth year, there was not a wrinkle on her face. She was just as fresh as she had been in the prime of her beauty"(Panas et al., 2012).

In order to appear youthful, it is likely Empress Zoe dyed her hair and spent a great deal of time applying cosmetics to lighten her skin. Two prominent physicians, Alexander of Tralles (6th century) and Paul of Aegina (7th century), refer in their works to the methods of dying hair. In order to dye the hair blond or red, herbs such as myrrh, lime, saffron, sandarach and golden herb are mixed with a fatty substance and applied to the head for one or two days (Panas et al., 2012). In order to achieve the most prominent feature of classic Greek and Roman beauty, pure white skin, native Greek, Roman and Byzantine women who were not naturally fair-skinned applied whitening make-up. In order to achieve the desired skin tone, the make-up usually contained white lead and chalked powder. Although aware of the poisonous attributes, women were willing to overlook the harm to obtain beauty (Panas et al., 2012).

The concept of youth often aligns very closely with beauty. The Byzantine women were willing to undergo painful and poisonous treatments to maintain their beauty, which is not entirely unlike treatments of more contemporary societies. During the life of Empress Zoe, the treatment to obtain eternal youth included seemingly extreme treatments using lead and chalk. The anti ageing methods of today, such as the previously mentioned cryotherapy, which researchers use to freeze off abnormal cells was eventually transformed into a tool to preserve youth (Hubbard, 2014). Without a doubt, such treatments required a great deal of research and trial and error in order to accomplish the lofty longevity goals of the modern world. Indeed, there are entire television shows following the result of botched surgeries and attempts to chase and capture eternal youth, a practice not dissimilar to the Mediterranian women of the Byzantine era. Each process involves unnatural alterations and has the potential to go horribly wrong. Historically, the appearance of youth well into old age held many parallels to longevity, and research conducted on Byzantine medical practices found cosmetic medicine made up a huge portion of the material (Panas et al., 2012). However, the obsession with beauty and eternal youth can not be considered the same as the desire for increased longevity. For Empress Zoe, the quest for eternal youth dominated her life, which is not the same as a desire for immortality or, more realistically, a life span much longer than average.

The search for longevity in the epic of Gilgamesh and the search for eternal youth by Empress Zoe are but two of many searches throughout history of those wanting to escape the effects of aging. Alexander the Great, who conquered many new lands during the fourth century BCE, is believed to have devoted time searching for a "river of paradise" to prevent ageing. In the fifth century BCE, the Greek historian Herodotus described a fountain responsible for extending the lives of the Macrobians, who lived in northern Africa in ancient times (Rohland, 2020). Beginning in the twelfth century CE, Europeans circulated a legend of a king named Prester John, supposedly ruling a kingdom containing not only a fountain of youth but also a river flowing with gold. Tales of hot springs capable of repairing injuries and reversing the ageing process have persisted in Japan for centuries (Rohland,

2020). This long tradition of attempting to escape the clutches of age and death persist today.

In addition to the anecdotes described above, one particularly well known legend is that of the Fountain of Youth. The Fountain of Youth is often initially associated with Juan Ponce de León, an explorer of parts of the Caribbean in the late fifteenth and early sixteenth centuries on behalf of Spain. Native inhabitants of various Caribbean islands reportedly shared accounts of a body of water (a river, a waterfall, a spring) that could transform adults into children. One alleged location was a lost land called Bimini, located north of Cuba and Haiti. According to legend, Ponce de León set out to search for this land to find the magical Fountain of Youth. In the process, he discovered present-day Florida, which he claimed for Spain and proceeded to explore. Some accounts claim that he first came ashore in St. Augustine, Florida, the oldest continuously inhabited European settlement in America. Other accounts indicate that he came ashore farther south in Melbourne, Florida. Regardless, Florida boasted many natural springs, and Ponce de León believed that one of them could be the Fountain of Youth. While searching for gold to claim on behalf of Spain, he also searched for the legendary fountain (Rohland, 2020).

Modern history scholars generally agree that Ponce de León's quest for the Fountain of Youth is more fiction than fact. Contracts between Ponce de León and the Spanish crown do not mention the Fountain of Youth, and few other records written by Ponce de León survive. Historians know that Ponce de León anchored his ship off the eastern shore of Florida on April 2, 1513, and began exploring land the next day. Eight years later, in 1521, he returned to Florida to attempt to build a colony. A Native American shot Ponce de León in the leg with an arrow, and the explorer died in Cuba shortly after that. So, why the association between the explorer and the legend? One of the first people to connect Ponce de León with the Fountain of Youth was Spanish historian Gonzalo Fernández de Oviedo y Valdés. Oviedo and Ponce de León did not get along. Oviedo's 1535 account of Ponce de León's explorations set out to discredit the explorer by claiming that he had foolishly searched for the Fountain of Youth in a vain attempt to cure sexual impotence. Later, historians continued to connect Ponce de León to a quest to find the Fountain of Youth. In the nineteenth century, when Spain ceded Florida to the United States, the legend of Ponce de León's quest became entrenched in history and even found its way into history textbooks. In the twenty-first century, the legend persists, if only because people still dream of a way to ensure their perpetual youth and vigour (Rohland, 2020).

The legend of Ponce de León's quest for the Fountain of Youth has lasted for centuries. Indeed, several towns in Florida purport to be the home of the "real" Fountain of Youth. One of the most well-known is St. Augustine. The fountain's association with "America's oldest city" began in the 1870s when a real estate promoter dubbed a small stream "Ponce de León Spring" and claimed that it was the Fountain of Youth. Today, St. Augustine is home to the Fountain of Youth Archaeological Park (Rohland, 2020). Thousands of tourists visit the park each year to learn about the Spanish settlers who founded the city and the Timucua people who lived there for nearly three thousand years before the settlers' arrival. For many, a highlight of the park tour is tasting water from a stone well identified as "The Fountain of Youth," but most visitors report that the water tastes a bit like rotten eggs (Rohland, 2020).

Modern historians generally agree that the Fountain of Youth and Ponce de León's quest to find it are the stuff of fantasy. Not to mention it had little impact on the search for eternal youth (Rohland, 2020). Less than a hundred years after Ponce de León's explorations for the Fountain of Youth, gruesome news emerged of the Hungarian countess Elizabeth Báthory, another said to have pursued prolonged youth (Pallardy, 2020). Married for the first time at eleven and again at fifteen, Báthory gave birth to five children, but only three survived to adulthood. Further records show her second husband, a skilled soldier, died in 1604, leaving Báthory with an impressive estate (Biography.com, 2020, Pallardy, 2020). After the death of her husband, the rumours began to circulate, suggesting Báthory used her status to lure young virgins to her estate. Specific accusations were made that Báthory, jealous and filled with hate, would coat her victims with honey and leave them outdoors for the insects to feast (Pallardy, 2020). Further tales recall the countess sometimes tortured girls by driving needles into their fingers, cutting their noses or lips or whipping them with stinging nettles. She would bite shoulders and breasts, as well as burning the flesh, including the genitals, of some victims (Pallardy, 2020).

Apparently, in addition to various torture methods, legends speculate Báthory would bathe in the blood of virgin maidens, in hopes of discovering her lost youth. Although there is no hard evidence to suggest Báthory bathed in the blood of virgins, written historical records recall Báthory's arrest in 1611; the trial documents reaffirm these accusations made against her (Biography.com, 2020, Pallardy, 2020). The legend of the Blood Countess should be considered carefully as the first mention of Bathory's blood baths came a hundred years after her death. Further, modern scholarship has questioned the allegations' veracity. This is because Báthory was a powerful woman, made more so by inheriting control of her husband's wealth. Further evidence suggests the Báthory family, aside from the countess, cancelled a large debt owed by a fellow noble, to the Báthorys in exchange for allowing them to control her in captivity. All of which suggests that the accusations were politically motivated slander that allowed relatives to appropriate her lands (Biography.com, 2020). While the countess was a wealthy and powerful noblewoman accused of horrifying age-defying rituals it is unlikely the legends reflect reality. (Pallardy, 2020) Then again, historical records show there may be some truth to the accusations. In 1602 a priest wrote a letter that discussed the excessive cruelty exhibited by Báthory and her husband towards their servants. The testimony against Báthory likely included true tales about how harshly she acted with lower classes. Such acts were not illegal at the time — Báthory was only punished because her victims were said to have included noblewomen — but would still make Báthory responsible for many ruined lives (Biography.com, 2020). Báthory would go on to be known as the Blood Countess and is often considered the inspiration for the Legend of Count Dracula. The legend of the virgin blood baths continued.

Today, the quest for longevity typically coincides with the much more attainable search for eternal youth. In late December of 2016, scientists at the Salk Institute for Biological Studies announced that they had found a way to reverse the signs of ageing in mice (Ocampo et al.). The process, called cellular reprogramming, extended the lives of the mice involved in the study and allowed them to live longer without experiencing the usual signs of ageing. For example, the reprogrammed mice lived about thirty percent longer than mice that had been allowed to age normally. The reprogrammed mice appeared younger and healthier and demonstrated improved organ function. The study has given scientists hope that they may one day achieve similar results in human subjects, although such experimentation would not likely occur for another decade. In Chapter 8, the concept of cellular reprogramming is discussed further as cellular manipulation. The study's success has led some to call cellular reprogramming a real "fountain of youth." (Rohland, 2020). Today, adding life to years cannot be viewed simply as a medical issue because the quality of a prolonged life depends on cognitive, behavioural, psychological, and social processes (Lang et al., 2019).

Chapter 2
Global Perspectives on Ageing, Youth & Vitality

"In ancient China, the Taoists taught that a constant inner smile, a smile to oneself, insured health, happiness and longevity. Why? Smiling to yourself is like basking in love: you become your own best friend. Living with an inner smile is to live in harmony with yourself."

- Mantak Chia

Introduction

The global perspective on youth, ageing and longevity began to shift during the Age of Enlightenment spanning the 17th and 18th centuries. Research conducted by Max Roser, Esteban Ortiz-Ospina, and Hannah Ritchie on global Life Expectancies explain that at the beginning of the 19th-century, the meaning of longevity did not exist in the same way as it does today. Today, the global life expectancy has more than doubled, with some countries having an average life expectancy of over 80 years old. While many resources are allocated toward anti-ageing technologies, perceptions of ageing continue to be somewhat harmful. Moreover, much of the insight into longevity is through a western lens, which is considered ethnocentric. This chapter will outline various global perspectives on ageing, longevity, youth and vitality. The perspectives outlined are gathered from various sources, and data pools, and therefore do not represent the feelings or opinions of individuals or the entire global population. Specifically, Western Perspectives, East Asian Taoist Perspectives, Mediterranean Perspectives, African Perspectives and Ashkenazi

Jewish Perspectives are addressed. Throughout the chapter, these five longevity, ageing and vitality perspectives will show how social, economic and cultural factors influence the understanding.

A desire to maintain youth and vitality is no shock in the modern world. Whether feeling spry into old age or undergoing anti-ageing cosmetic procedures, the path to increased life span and the desire to control the ageing process has changed. The global perspective on youth, ageing and longevity began to shift during the Age of Enlightenment. They were fueled by the Industrial Revolution, which began in the 18th century. Life expectancies in hubs of innovation began to rise while the less fortunate fell behind. Research conducted by Max Roser, Esteban Ortiz-Ospina, and Hannah Ritchie (2013) on global Life Expectancies explains that at the beginning of the 19th-century, the meaning of longevity did not exist in the same way as it does today. People across the globe did not expect to live past 40 years old. Whereas, today, the global life expectancy has more than doubled, with some countries having an average life expectancy of over 80 years old (Roser et al., 2013). While medical, technical and social developments have provided numerous positive factors associated with a global increase in longevity, the result is not without consequences (Lang et al., 2019). Ultimately, limited research has been conducted on anti-ageing and longevity cross-cultural perspectives, making available research limited in scope but considerably in-depth. In other words, the available resources contain a great deal of information on a select number of countries, thus shining a bright light on perspectives of interest to the researcher and the author, rather than encompassing the global population in its entirety. Consequently, any global perspectives discussed can be understood as assumptions formed from a limited data set. With this in mind, the perspectives may offer a new way to grow older and maintain youth.

Alarming data collected on country-specific life expectancy in the last 100 years found that people in India and South Korea were expected to live as little as 23 years (Rice & Fineman, 2004). While later than the rest of the world, life expectancy in South Korea eventually caught up and eventually surpassed countries like Japan and the U.K. (Roser et al., 2013). However, people in the U.K. live more than twice as long as they did at the beginning of the 19th century, with the life expectancy averaging at just over 80 in the year 2019 (Roser et al., 2013). While living longer may seem like a problem-free way to defeat a natural lifespan, the reality was that declining death rates and increased life expectancy would cause problems for countries that underwent a baby boom (Ekerdt et al., 2017). After all, this is because while people are living longer, they are not necessarily living well.

While many resources are allocated toward anti-ageing technologies, perceptions of ageing continue to be somewhat harmful. In 1939, Piersol and Bortz argued, "… it is for science to add life to years and not years to life" (Piersol G. M., & Bortz E. L, 1939 as cited by Lang et al., 2019, p. 1). What Piersol and Bortz suggest is that modern science need not concern itself with longevity. Instead, the focus should be on making improvements to the average life span. Western societies place a great deal of emphasis on youth and vitality and tend to dismiss or have a distaste towards ageing (Löckenhoff et al., 2009, p. 942). Thus cross-cultural research on perceptions of ageing and longevity has focused primarily on the differences in perceptions held by individuals within Western cultures. Research conducted on the impact of ageing cultural values on society has focused primarily on comparing Eastern/Asian to Western cultures (Löckenhoff. et al., 2009). Therefore much of the insight into longevity is through a western lens which is considered ethnocentric. Ethnocentrism is the evaluation of a culture based on the biases and standards of one's own culture. However, Löckenhoff et al. conducted research on "Perceptions of Aging Across 26 Cultures and Their Culture-Level Associates" found widespread agreement toward the impact of ageing on personal characteristics (Löckenhoff et al., 2009, p. 949). In other words, across 26 cultures, people agree that aspects such as wisdom typically come with age.

As we age, there are other not-so-pleasant results, such as an increased economic burden and fractured social connections (Ekerdt et al., 2017). This makes sense considering research conducted in Germany, China and the United States on whether longevity is a value to adults 65 and over found that over one-third of the 90 participants expressed zero goals for longer life. Individuals with no intention to increase their life were found to hold the belief that their life had run their natural course. In other words, the refusal was essentially considered a form of fate acceptance (Ekerdt et al., 2017). The people who did not express the desire to increase their lifespan are unique. Most people would jump at the chance to add years to their life. Interestingly, wanting to live as long as one expects reflects an acceptance of the finitude of one's natural life. A desire to live much longer than one expects to live may indicate a desire to overcome the actual limits of life expectancy. A wish to live shorter than expected may imply a negative or deprecating attitude toward ageing. (Lang et al., 2019).

Further findings from "Is Longevity A Value For Older Adults?" found diversity in the ideal length of life and various elements linked to ranging perspectives toward ageing and longevity. In general, when asked, individuals seem to value health over sheer longevity (Ekerdt et al., 2017). In other words, people do not want to live forever if they are sick or incapacitated. Nevertheless, in order to classify perspectives held on longevity, researchers Lang and Rupprecht (2019) used existing theoretical and empirical data to identify three cross-cultural perspectives. First, the essentialist mindset builds on the principles of eternal life. Those who conform to the essentialist mindset wish to entirely or seriously postpone the ageing process. The second mindset presented is the medical mindset which values longevity based on physical health. In other words, long life is only worth living if one is healthy and able-bodied. Lastly, the stoicism mindset understands longevity as closely connected to the experience of grace and meaning. Lang and Rupprecht (2019) argue that the "motivation for longevity and its behavioural consequences differ depending on what mindsets individuals adopt in a given developmental context" (p.1).

Lang & Rupprecht argue that perspectives toward longevity are rooted in a person's belief system. In other words, people have opinions stemming from their unique understanding of the world. Beliefs are a combination of what one may perceive as right or wrong, values, traditions, religious, political or social understandings typically established over a lifetime. To illustrate, some people may attribute a longer life exclusively to the biomedical advances of the modern world. Biomedical advances, in other words, are innovations in the biological, medical, and physical sciences. Advancements in these fields have prompted some people to believe the key to longevity is found exclusively in medical, biological and physical innovations modified for cosmetic and medical services. However, individuals who believe longevity is primarily due to biomedical advancements tend to believe longevity is only worthwhile if they are healthy and independent. That is to say, in order for a long life to have value, one must live an independent life free from illness or institutions. In contrast, others consider life a series of accomplishments. These individuals believe additional years should be filled with learning and personal growth. Accomplishments include mastering the violin or a new language, essentially the pursuit of personal fulfillment.

However, most overlook the health, financial and social components of longevity. For example, along with a longer life, individuals should expect to lose friends and family members to the natural elements. Furthermore, with age comes an increased chance of illness and more expenses than those who live an average or below average lifespan. Heath inevitably deteriorates and with decreasing health and a longer life comes increased expenses to maintain the vitality required to continue past the average life span. Therefore, those who accept a natural life span may appear more rational than those who believe otherwise. Unsurprisingly, the research found more than half of the participants expressed a desire to extend their lifespan, though less than half could give an estimated amount of time (Ekerdt et al., 2017). Lang & Rupprecht (2019), in the article titled "Motivation for Longevity Across the Life Span: An Emerging Issue," explain that ageing may involve the need to accept personal vulnerability. In other words, the desire for longevity may come from a fear of the unknown—alternatively, an inability to accept the certainty of death, which is understandably terrifying to many. Consequently, psychological resilience to adverse life conditions may foster long-term motivation for longevity from early adulthood until very late in life (Lang & Rupprecht, 2019). In other words, individuals who can navigate stress and hardship well may be more likely to desire a long life, particularly one that is longer than average. Longer life for people who are resilient and adaptable would obviously be much more fulfilling than an individual troubled by change.

The previously mentioned research conducted by Löckenhoff et al. (2009) on college students across 26 cultures evaluated perceptions toward ageing populations. According to a method cited by Löckenhoff. et al., on forming collective cognition social representations theory, "the views of ageing held within a given culture are a form of shared cultural representation" (Moscovici, 1984, 1988 as cited by Löckenhoff. et al., 2009, p.4). Thereby emphasizing an expectation for potential variations in perspectives cross-culturally. Löckenhoff et al. (2009) note additional studies that the treatment of ageing populations vary. All are concluding that the perceptions of ageing create shared values, expectations and responses toward ageing (Löckenhoff. et al., 2009). Perspectives formed in society on ageing can be understood as social constructions. Socially constructed views are established and accepted but not necessarily established using the scientific method. Consequently, societies across the globe may have firm perspectives on youth, ageing, and longevity that are entirely unfounded. Lang & Rupprecht (2019) argue that health and culture influence diverse global perspectives toward prolonged life, such as the specific desire to postpone death.

However, with an increasing number of people experiencing extended life spans, many also come to appreciate the potential for the additional years to be pleasant, even when conditions are not excellent. Therefore, adding life to years is not simply a medical issue because the quality of a prolonged life also depends on cognitive, behavioural, psychological, and social processes (Lang & Rupprecht, 2019). The following portion of the chapter will outline various global perspectives on ageing, longevity, youth and vitality. The perspectives outlined are gathered from a variety of sources, and data pools, therefore, do not represent the feelings or opinions of individuals. In other words, just because someone is from a specific region, they do not hold a specific perspective by default.

Western Perspectives

Western perspectives include European cultures (Croatia, Czech Republic, Estonia, France, Great Britain, Poland, Portugal, the Russian Federation, Serbia, Slovakia, and Switzerland) and the United States, Canada, New Zealand and Australia (Löckenhoff. et al., 2009, p. 11). Ageing is a process that continues over the entire life span, but the rate of ageing varies considerably among individuals and population groups (Rice & Fineman, 2004, p 458). Americans specifically are living longer than ever before. Improvements in living conditions and lifestyles, as well as advances in science, technology, medicine and pharmaceuticals, have resulted in significant reductions in morbidity and mortality from previously fatal infectious diseases, dramatic increases in life expectancy, and a rapid increase in the number of older Americans (Rice & Fineman, 2004, p 458). According to the U.S Census Bureau estimates, by the year 2050 one out of five Americans will be 65 and over (Liu, 2013). Ageing populations have an undeniable implication on the cost of healthcare. Specifically, a growing ageing population puts pressure on the social and economic institutions of a society.

A survey conducted in the United States by the CDC in 2018 found the average American should expect to live till roughly 78, with the female population expecting to live till an average of 81.2 and the males till 76.2 (CDC, 2018, p. 1). According to a survey conducted by the Pew Research Center "Living to 120 and Beyond: Americans' Views on Aging, Medical Advances and Radical Life Extension," Americans seem to have high hopes for old age but are not generally interested in dramatically increasing their lifespan. Specifically, the study found 81% of people satisfied with life as is and 56% think things will only get better or will stay the same (28%) (Liu, 2013, p. 10). Thus it appears people are not overly concerned with improving their lifestyle as they age. Evidently, the survey found two-thirds of Americans ages 65 and older fully expect their lives to be better (23%) or about the same (43%) in the next decade. Further demonstrating that a great deal of the American ageing population are optimistic about ageing. In contrast, 18% of respondents expressed "a lot." 23% say they worry "a little" about outliving their financial resources in retirement, more than half (57%) say they either do not worry "too much" about this or do not worry about it "at all (Liu, 2013, p. 10).

Participants of "Living to 120 and Beyond: Americans' Views on Aging, Medical Advances and Radical Life Extension" were asked if they would want medical treatments that slow the ageing process and allow them to live decades longer, to at least 120 years old, about four-in-ten U.S. adults (38%) say they would, while more than half (56%) say they would not. By contrast, about seven in ten (68%) speculate that most people would want such treatments, while roughly a quarter (27%) say most people would not want them. Not surprisingly, personal desire for life-extending treatments is closely related to views about their overall effect on society. Of those who say such treatments would be suitable for society, 71% say they would want to receive them. Conversely, the overwhelming majority (83%) of those who think such treatments would be a bad thing for society say they personally would not want medical treatments to slow the ageing process and live decades longer.

In general, western societies do not tend to portray ageing in a favourable light. For example, media tabloids and television show slander ageing people, particularly ageing women. A report titled Media Image Landscaping published by the AARP describes the images commonly projected by the media in the U.S. However, the media patterns displayed by the U.S are similar to those held in other westernized cultures (Thayer & Skufca 2019). Unsurprisingly, people over 50 are rarely seen on television or, oddly, are rarely shown using technology. However, Thayer & Skufca (2019) argue that people over 50 lack independence and are technologically inept. Further, many media representations of the ageing population exclude them from the workplace or have significant financial status. Thus, the lack of representation has implications for the ageing population in that it reinforces negative stereotypes. The media heavily influence perspectives toward ageing populations. Therefore, images that portray ageing people as isolated or dependent frames ageing in an understandably negative light. The media has an essential role in the perspectives held in western societies toward ageing, youth and longevity. Without a doubt, people are interested in prolonging life and stunting ageing in Westernized countries. However, this could be partly due to the subtle yet detrimental stereotypes portaged by various elements of Westernized culture.

East Asian Taoist Perspectives

In the history of East Asia, Taoism became the most influential spiritual or philosophical tradition in the development of traditional Chinese medicine, affecting its philosophy, theory, terminology, and practice. Taoism is one of many Eastern cultural traditions that greatly respect the elderly. In contrast to modern westernized societies that tend to dismiss ageing members of society. The founder Chinese philosopher named Lao Zi means "Old Gentleman." The legend tells his mother held him in her stomach for ten years, and when he was born, he was an older person. The legend is indicating great respect for an older person who cultivates the knowledge of the Dao throughout life. According to the Dao, the wise old man is a symbol to be respected. The respect for ageing in Taoist tradition is particularly due to its appreciation of dialectic thinking and the wisdom accumulated with old age (Ai, 2006, p. 156). Dialectic thinking can be understood as the ongoing art of investigation, growth and the pursuit of wisdom. According to Taoist spirituality, as a person ages, they must practice self-care and energy exercise rather than seek biomedical treatments (Ai, 2006, p. 156). Interestingly, Taoist is often practiced by many individuals as they age throughout Chinese history. According to Taoist philosopher Zhuang Zi, longevity can be obtained through energy movement and deep breath. Through this early practice of qigong, called Dao-yin two thousand years ago. Qigong is a form of martial arts focused on breath, posture, movement and concentration, which according to Taoist spirituality, will contribute to increased health and longevity.

> *"Exhaling through the mouth while exercising the breath,*
> *Spitting out the old breaths, drawing in the new,*
> *Moving like the bear, stretching like the bird,*
> *This is simply the art of longevity.*
> *As the aim of those scholars who practice dao-yin. (Zi, as cited by Ai, 2006, p. 157)* "

East Asian Taoist perspectives toward longevity are less concerned with quantity and more so with quality. In other words, Taoism accepts that death is inescapable and challenges the past and present negative images of death that do not provide holistic care for the dying. Care for the dying and respect are essential in the Taoist understanding of ageing (Ai, 2006, p. 158). Interestingly, Lao Zi offers a Taoist attitude toward death. In other words, Taoism spirituality includes the element of an immortal soul in the form of spiritual immortality (Ai, 2006, p.

158). Therefore, East Asian Taoist perspectives toward longevity encompass spiritual and metaphysical elements. Specifically, that eternal life comes with a spiritual unity and merging with the universal law, or the Dao (Ai, 2006, p. 158).

Mediterranean Perspectives

Mediterranean people are understood as individuals who come from countries touching the mediterranean sea. Spain, France, Monaco, Italy, Croatia, Greece, Syria, Turkey, Egypt and many more fall under the umbrella of the Mediterranean. Many countries border the mediterranean sea, it is important to note the cultures are vast, and it is wrong to assume each individual who resides near the sea will share the same perspectives. Further, you will note as you continue, there is overlap in countries within Mediterranean and Western perspectives. People are complex beings and have the potential to hold multifaceted perspectives toward complex issues such as ageing, longevity and eternal life. Further, perspectives are not unanimously held by individuals born in a specific geographical region. Rather, individual cultural, age and social groups tend to share similar perspectives toward ageing (Löckenhoff. et al., 2009). Historically, Greeks did not consider themselves in control of their lifespan. Rather ageing and longevity were under the control of the gods. Death and destruction were seen as supernatural forces and could be a result of a particular god or group of gods. Nevertheless, this was a crucial element to the way Ancient Greeks understood heath, ageing and longevity (Finch, 2010; p. 358).

Ancient Greek poet Homer bestowed upon civilization some of the only insight available into early Greek perspectives toward ageing and longevity. Finch (2010) explains Homer emphasized diet as linked to longevity and eternal life. Specifically, the gods ate only ambrosia and nectar, and would not touch grains and wine, the subsistence of the mortals. Therefore, suggesting diet is essential to longevity. Moreoso, the poetry of Homer provides a fragment of insight into the value ancient Greeks placed on nutrition. So much so that Homer used it to separate mortals from the gods (p. 358). Unsurprisingly, various studies have found a Mediterranean diet may have the potential to impact longevity. In other words, it is a commonly held perspective in Mediterranean cultures that diet has an impact on ageing.

While the components of a Mediterranean diet have changed over time, a small number of foods have remained constant. Early Greek mythology contains repetitive mention of three foods gifted to mortals by Greek Goddesses Demeter, Athena and Dionysus. Specifically, bread, oil and wine represent a culture founded on living off the land since these products do not exist in nature by themselves but instead have to be made by using and combining locally grown ingredients. Mediterranean food culture was in contrast with the uncivilized food production of meat, lard and butter. Nevertheless, after the fall of the Roman Empire, the early Greek people eventually shared the foods with the Romans, resulting in the co-production of animal and plant products we understand as the modern model for food consumption (Vasto et al., 2014). Shifting away from the spiritual aspects, the high level of antioxidants and essential fatty acids in the Mediterranean diet has been found to reduce the risk of cardiovascular disease, cancer and other degenerative diseases attributed to the nutraceutical effect of micronutrients and compounds with the capacity of antithrombotic anticancer and antioxidants (di Daniele et al., 2016). In other words, the Mediterranean diet has been found to assist in the prevention and reduction of blood clots, increase absorption of nutrients, may contribute to a healthier heart and a decreased risk of cancer. Fish products and extra virgin olive oil are mainly responsible for the contribution of essential fatty acids and oleic acid (di Daniele et al., 2016). Today individuals all over the world have begun to jump on various trends in order to live longer healthier lives, including the Mediterranean diet. While spirituality is deeply intertwined with the diet, modern science has shown without a doubt the Mediterranean diet contributes to longevity, health and vitality. As a result, rightly so, those who border the mediterranean sea have held the common belief for centuries that eating specific foods will contribute to a longer life.

African Perspectives

There are 54 countries in Africa; a thorough understanding of the ageing and longevity perspectives held in this continent would require an entire book of its own. Moreover, much of the research and understanding of Africa as a continent is framed through a colonialist lens or is heavily focused on elements of poverty. Thankfully there was available research conducted on the ageing populations in sub-Saharan Africa that has been done by an African and American research collaboration. The article titled "Aging in Sub-Saharan Africa: Recommendation for Furthering Research" places a great deal of emphasis on understanding the situation of older people, longevity, health, and wellness in sub-Saharan Africa. Research on longevity and ageing perspectives held in various countries within Africa is scarce due to the vast geographical region; the variation in perspectives can be partially attributed to physical geography, climate, culture, tradition, beliefs, religions and value systems (Cohen & Menken, 2006). Further, as mentioned research conducting on ageing includes a discussion of the socioeconomic status of the region rather than the perspectives gathered through interaction with the population. Thus it is no surprise researchers found older people in sub-Saharan Africa were primarily concerned with practical issues rather than focused on increased longevity or eternal youth. Specifically, researchers emphasized that attention is more often aimed toward the proportion of households unable to provide themselves with basic food and nonfood items (Cohen & Menken, 2006, p.1). Moreover, Cohen & Menken (2006) explain that sub-Saharan African societies are expected to cope with an ageing population and a catastrophic health crisis without a universal formal social security system or a well-functioning traditional care system. Furthermore in the past two decades, vitality, health, and longevity in sub-Saharan Africa have been dramatically influenced by HIV/AIDS (Cohen & Menken 2006, p. 89). According to Cohen & Menken (2006), in the year 2004, over two million people died of AIDS, and they estimated by 2020, over 75 million Africans will have lost their lives to AIDS since the beginning of the epidemic. While the estimation made by Cohen & Menken is high, the reality is anti-ageing and longevity as aspirations are rare in regions that are surviving colonization, poverty and disease.

Ashkenazi Jewish Perspectives

Various studies have been conducted on the secret to exceptional longevity, many of which mention the persistence of Ashkenazi Jews. Historically, Ashkenazi are members of the Jewish faith who adopted the German synagogue ritual rather than the Spanish rituals of the Sephardic Jews (Britannica, 2020). According to Encyclopedia Britannica (2020), Ashkenazim make up more than 80% of the Jewish population sitting at about 11 million at the beginning of the 21st century. Work done by Barzilai and colleagues at the Institute for Aging Research, Diabetes Research and Training Center titled "Unique Lipoprotein Phenotype and Genotype Associated With Exceptional Longevity" researched "213 Ashkenazi Jewish probands" and their children from 1998 to 2002. Proband is a term used to describe the first people participating in a genetic medical or psychiatric study of a family (Barzilai et al., 2003, p. 2030). Thus, the study aimed to discover any specific biological and genetic markers linked to longevity.

Moreover, to identify any observable characteristics specific to Ashkenazi people resulting from a genetic response to environmental factors linked to longevity (Barzilai et al., 2003, p. 2030). The questionnaire, physical examinations and blood tests were done. Researchers assessed lipids and lipoproteins subclass levels and particle sizes by proton nuclear magnetic resonance. Lipids are organic compounds that are fatty acids or their derivatives and can not be dissolved in water but can be dissolved by other organic solvents. For example, natural oils, waxes and steroids are classified as lipids. Lipoproteins are the dissolvable proteins that combine and transport fat or other lipids in the blood plasma. Thus the research conducted by Barzilai et al. (2003) found high-density lipoproteins (HDL) and low-density lipoprotein (LDL) particle sizes were more prominent in the Ashkenazi Jewish population than in the control groups. Control groups being made up of non-Ashkenazi individuals in order to establish a baseline.

Further, the HDL and LDL were notably higher in the children without hypertension or cardiovascular disease. In general, the most impressive findings were that individuals with exceptional longevity and their children were found to have much higher HDL and LDL particle sizes. The presentation of larger particle sizes is often associated with decreased rates of hypertension, heart disease, metabolic syndrome. As well as a richer likelihood, the genes responsible for the cholesteryl ester transfer protein (CETP) I405V variant will be inherited by future generations. Bustami et al. (2016) explain that the CETP is a plasma protein that catalyzes cholesteryl ester transfer from HDL to other lipoproteins. CETP I405V variant was critical to larger high-density lipoprotein, low-density lipoprotein particle sizes and lower rates of hypertension, metabolic syndrome, and cardiovascular disease (Barzilai et al., 2003; Newman & Murabito, 2013; Bustami et al., 2016). Hence, the children of Ashkenazi Jews can inherit lipoprotein particle sizes, resulting in healthy ageing and, consequently, increased longevity.

"The Epidemiology of Longevity and Exceptional Survival" by Ann Newman and Joanne Murabito (2013) outlines numerous studies dedicated to understanding longevity. While epidemiology typically deals with the prevalence and distribution of diseases, Newman and Murabito describe the research on the environmental, social and biological factors that may contribute to longevity. Unsurprisingly, studies show that Ashkenazi Jews 95 and over living without assistance did not appear to be different from the general population of the same birth cohort concerning lifestyle factors such as diet, physical activity, and body mass index (Rajpathak et al., 2011). Thus providing further evidence of the critical role genetics may have on longevity. Specific research conducted on the Ashkenazi personal perspectives on why they have exceptional longevity found one-third considered family history or good genetics an essential factor (Rajpathak et al., 2011). However, women were more likely than men to report good genetics. Men were more likely to perceive longevity as a result of a healthy diet. An average of 20% of participants believed exercise contributed to a longer life; however, being positive (18.8%), family support (17.5%) or an acti ve life (11.6%)

were also included as perceived factors contributing to longevity (Rajpathak et al., 2011).

The above perspectives are only a few of the possible understandings of longevity. According to research conducted by Dumas and Turner (2015) on Human Longevity, Utopia and Solidarity, the political economy of representation recognizes scarcity as a critical issue in the politics of longevity. Dumas and Turner demonstrate that scientific revolutions in biotechnologies and information technology will not overcome inequalities in distribution and may considerably increase inequality. Specifically, research has begun to suggest that older people in modern-day biotechnological and consumer cultures will be frequently compelled to adopt a more thoughtful approach to longevity by considering the risks and benefits of how they want to experience their ageing bodies (Dumas & Turner, 2015, p.5). Dumas & Turner (2015) further explain that emerging consumer markets and biomedicine produce a highly seductive antiaging rhetoric and related technologies that have resulted in a growing interest in the medicalization and commercialization of age and ageing. Further, the shifting interest is slowly but surely redefining the relationship between old age and society.

Nevertheless, these techno-economic changes have caused new areas of vulnerability masked by the medical utopia of good health and living eternally. The antiaging dialogues shadow broader social solidarity and political economy issues by responding to statements that longevity can be framed regarding the relations among scarcity, human vulnerability, and precariousness of social institutions. Humans have been distinguished by vulnerability throughout history, in which we share the inevitable aspects of humanity; suffering, illness, and death (Dumas & Turner, 2015). In response, humankind creates institutions to build a shared environment where their vulnerability can be reduced but not eliminated. Hence, humans rely on institutions rather than nature to survive because humanity exists in an environment inevitably plagued by security (Dumas & Turner, 2015). Considering the desire for a longer life is undoubtedly an established and commonly held perspective across the globe. Researchers Dumas and Turner argue that ethical and religious concerns are likely only to be considered once the harmful impact of longevity is in full swing (Dumas & Turner, 2015, p. 7). Thus long life and health are entirely possible, at least by the control of institutions and corporations who promote the possibility of longevity (Dumas & Turner, 2015, p. 14).

While there are dozens of opinions on longevity, it is without a doubt that technological advancements are elongating the natural life span. However, longevity is not a global phenomenon. Specifically, while youth is valued to some degree in every part of the world, we see the drive toward longer, better lives in wealthy westernized countries. Nevertheless, there has been an inevitable focus on adding years rather than on the concept of 'living and ageing well.' As mentioned at the beginning of the chapter, just because one lives longer does not necessarily mean they will have their health, family or finances. With age comes specific needs, and while in western cultures there is a growing ageing population and a profound disregard for the less fortunate. There is an obvious issue that stems from glorifying youth, therefore we must instead encourage a shift in focus to ensure the global population has the potential to age gracefully.

Chapter 3
Social Impacts of Anti-Ageing

"Ethnic culture is broadly defined as a multidimensional construct represented by values, identity, race, religious orientation, immigrant status, and nationality."

- Blieszner & Bedford

Introduction

The 'family model' is varied and intersectional in the 21st century. As communities across the globe continue to integrate and interact, the change in conceptions of family dynamics continue to speed up. This chapter attempts to approach and describe how elements of family-member longevity shape the lives of families across the world, while recognizing that consideration of these variables permeates nearly all aspects of how families across culture and geography function. We also present subjective speculations on how anti-aging trends and technologies predicate familial impacts across geographic and cultural contexts.

Longevity and Lifespan vs Anti-Aging: Impacts on Families

Ethnicity and culture are powerful contextual influencers, impacting the intergenerational experiences of families across the world. That is, ethnicity and culture impact aging-related processes and customs that bare influence on how families operate according to their unique contextual circumstances (Blieszner &

Bedford, 2012). Specific examples of this broad contextual impact may include determining how young and old family members are cared for, familial roles, hierarchical identities determined by age, and the procurement of resources and shelter. Ethnicity and culture, including nativity and nationality, often create intergenerational variances that, when intertwined with forces such as need and scarcity, create 'norms' that have consequences for a family's well being and that of its constituent individuals.

Age carries a widespread importance in cross-cultural conceptions of family. Paradoxically, the 'duty to care' for a family's young, often prescribed to older family members, is sometimes superimposed by necessity for older individuals to be cared for by their young. The line between fiduciary and beneficiary is in perpetual flux due to variances in culture, ethnicity, and time. Blieszner and Bedford assert that the duty ascribed to individuals in a family is determined by a form of cultural capital called familialism. Conceptually, familism is a resource that families rely on to mitigate urgent needs of its members. One can assert that familialism plays a large role in determining whether family members of 'old' age are care-takers, or cared-for, as familialism represents a tangible taking of initiative.

It is worthwhile to note that familialism, the commitment to serving dependent family members, is not solely a byproduct of culture and ethnicity. Familialism is tethered to a given family's relationship to complex socioeconomic forces like social inequality, systematic racism, and capital wealth. These forces may necessitate and challenge caregivers in a given society, therefore subjugating the variable 'age' as an auxiliary consideration in determining who-does-what insofar as servitude within the family (Blieszner & Bedford, 2012). As a result, families that more heavily rely on familial servitude from younger members tend to experience a more dramatic reorganization of responsibilities as young family members age. These families often rely on a cultural expectation that young family members will grow-up to produce grand-children, and great-grand-children by a certain age in order to maintain continuity and socioeconomic security for the family unit (Lynch, 2016).

Through analysis of these sources we can speculate that the consequences imbued by the aging process are pace-dependent as impacted by necessity, scarcity, culture, and ethnicity. Social, economic, and geographic forces impact how quickly, and to what extent, family members take on familial responsibilities as they age. Aging therefore has diffuse impacts - ranging from increasing familial demands on younger family members who have a larger stake in caregiving and resource procurement (for example - asian, central american, south american cultures), and extending to old and elderly family members maintaining their roles as primary providers and caregivers into late-adulthood and old-age, for example - european descendant north-americans, african-americans, and western europeans. (Blieszner & Bedford, 2012).

With regard to health and longevity, the latter practice of maintaining primary familial roles - namely deferring retirement to provide for the family, presents potential challenges and benefits for one's longevity. In evaluating the broad diaspora of research on longevity and retirement, there is no clearly demarcated conclusion as to a general effect of retirement on health and longevity. Rather, a variety of conclusions have been drawn about specific contextual instances in which retirement may either promote, or hinder longevity (Hernaes, 2013). Inevitably, the contexts that determine these benefits and detractors are the social determinants of ethnicity and culture - that is to say, much of the research suggests that age of retirement in itself is not a barometer for evaluating one's prospected health or longevity. Rather, the type of lifestyle one engages in, or is subjected to, after deciding to retire ultimately reflects mortality prospects. As one might expect, ethnicity and culture play a penultimate role in determining lifestyle attributes of retirees - and thus, health related quality of life outcomes and life expectancy for older family members (Waldron, 2001).

For example, research from the University of Zurich in 2010 attempted to consider a causal relationship between retirement and mortality for blue-collar workers in Austria. The researchers focused on Austria in their study because of a change in unemployment insurance rules that allowed for some workers to retire up to 3.5 years earlier. This rule only applied in certain regions of Austria, allowing the U of Z research team to overcome endogenous selection bias while still maintaining relatively consistent cultural and ethnic compareters within the general Austrian population (Andreas K, et al, 2019). The study concludes that Austrian men who retire one-year earlier than the statutory retirement age (65), were 1.47% points more likely to die before age 73, which equates to a relative increase of 5.5% overall (Kuhn, et al, 2019). Meanwhile, early retirement in austrian women was not associated with worse health or mortality outcomes. The authors of the study assert that austrian women may cope more effectively with major life events, opt less-often for unhealthy post-retirement lifestyle changes, and suffer less intensely from a perceived loss of social status than retired Austrian men (Kuhn, et al, 2019). As is consistent with previous findings on the importance of cultural and ethnic context on mortality, older Austrian male family members who choose to retire early from blue-collar professions, a trend becoming more pronounced in contemporary western and central european societies, may suffer from a loss of health and longevity (Kuhn, et al, 2019).

Conversely, a conjoint effort led by researchers from the Ragnar Frisch Centre for Economic Research in Norway, and the University of New South Wales (Australia), found dissimilar results when attempting to quantify a relationship between retirement age and mortality in Norwegians. By taking advantage of new exclusionary retirement policy changes in Norway, the researchers analyzed mortality outcomes of norwegians eligible for early retirement against norwegians who were not. Unlike the University of Zurich study on Austrian retirement and mortality, the study on Norweiganers rendered no effect on mortality according to retirement age (Hernaes E, 2013). One might speculate from these findings that social and occupational determinants of health in Norway protect norwegians from health-deteriorating effects of working in later life for familial reasons - although, that is not a common familial archetype in Norway - evidenced by a scrupulous national social-safety net. (cite)

The above examples are not intended to speak on behalf of all cultural and ethnic contexts on the matter of working-age and longevity. Rather, they are a simple illustration of how elements of ethnicity and culture influence longevity from the perspective of highly variable, yet global familial norms; work and retirement.

Another notable, yet less contextually conscientious angle to observe work-longevity relationships from is that of biometrics. In 2020, the Clemson University (USA) department of economics and George Mason University (USA) School of Policy and Government published a revision of their work on retirement-related health biomarkers in American workers and retirees.

Biomarkers tested on the subjects included Body Mass Index (indicator for excess body fat), waist circumference (indicator for excess abdominal fat - correlated with metabolic complications), fasting blood sugar and Glycated Hemoglobin (diabetes), Blood Pressure, Triglycerides and HDL & LDL Cholesterol (heart disease), and high sensitivity C-reactive protein (tests for inflammation in the body) (Gorry, 2021).

Other chapters in this book will more-closely detail the age-related biometrics that are important in considering anti-aging and longevity. For the purpose of this chapter, it is most important to note that the aforementioned 2021 study from Gorry and colleagues observed highly varied biometric outcomes in retirees that both affirms early retirement as a potent longevity producer, and subsequently condemns early retirement as a longevity retractor with contraindicating biomarker results (Gorry, 2021). However, when measuring the biomarkers against participant's subjective health measures - the two data sets have polarizing features. Retiring appears to have a beneficial effect on subjective health measures. This means that despite certain biomarkers indicating a decrease in health and longevity after retirement, study participants who retired earlier reported feeling much healthier, leading to an opinion that their subjective health improvements may allow them to live longer (Gorry, 2021). The authors of this study assert that the discrepancy between self-report measures and biomarkers is consistent with the results of other empirical research conducted in the international community.

Impacts on Different Religions and Cultures

The essence of this chapter relies on the adoption of a stubborn, but foundational understanding; culture and ethnicity are contextual precursors that underpin population effects consequent from aging. This sentiment has been imbued ad nauseum, and will continue to be reiterated in the coming chapters. The most productive strategy to illustrate this principle's omnipresence is by providing examples demonstrating how cultures perpetuate unique relationships with vitality in the terminal context of aging.

It is not uncommon in 'western' cultures (read: western european & precipitates of european colonists on appropriated land) to evade the processes and perceptions of aging through pursuit of anti-aging products, philosophies, and marketing. The vast economic potential of marketing this type of vitality triggered the creation of a 2002 report from over 50 american researchers in the field of ant-aging to illuminate misinformation in the oversaturated anti-aging marketplace (Lim, 2004) - more on that later.

Kalyani K Mehta - associate professor of Psychology and Social Work at the National University of Singapore, differentiated and categorized patterns of age-conception between Indian, Malay, and Chinese ethnicities; The Chinese Pragmatic Pattern, Malay Religious Pattern, and Indian Spiritual Pattern. While this paper certainly makes a compelling case for the existence of differing cultural viewpoints on ageing, there is research that approaches this context far more encompassingly.

According to a behemoth paper published in the journal 'Psychology and Aging' in 2009, perceptions of aging can be traced to a variety of modern, premodern, and ancient cultural sources. The paper 'Perceptions of Aging Across 26 Cultures and Their Culture-Level Associates' by Lockenhoff et al, argues that there are clear distinctions between cultural notions of aging - something we would come to expect with our newfound appreciation of culture and ethnicity in this context. However, the paper also makes a strong case for the existence of stable cross-cultural perceptions of aging - seemingly universal across the 26 cultures examined by the study's authors - 49 in total.

Post-secondary students from six continents completed a pre-screening cultural identity inventory and read an information package about the study before committing their participation. The researchers created a 'perceptions of aging measure' or POA that displayed a list of age related perceptions, notions and ideals that could be understood by differing cultural identities. The authors explicitly state that their proprietary scale wasn't necessarily internally consistent. Rather, the items are intended to be viewed as related concepts that reflect cross-cultural thought patterns about aging and age-related associates (Lockenhoff et al, 2009). Participants answered questions about their culture's perceptions of aging precipitants and consequences such as physical appearance, potential for learning, general knowledge, familial authority, and wisdom (Lockenhoff et al, 2009).

Culture-level associates were also measured and intercorrelated with perceptions of aging gathered by the intercultural POA measure. These culture-level associates are complex, warranting explanations that transcend the practical boundaries of this chapter. For the sake of lay explanation, these associates included socioeconomic indicators, affective autonomy, intellectual autonomy, traditional values, secular-national values, and national character stereotypes - individual perceptions on how members of their culture act in accordance with stereotypes of that culture (Lockenhoff et al, 2009).

One would expect that results from this kind of research could be heavily skewed by the gender-identities of the respondents - an issue that may require amelioration when performing relevant statistical analyses. Ironically enough, several cultures had only male or female respondents, prompting the researchers to place even heavier emphasis on the relationship between gender and cultural perceptions than was originally planned. In the case of India, for example, the data analysis required consideration of disequal gender distribution because the respondents were all female (Lockenhoff et al, 2009).

The overall results from the study are encompassed in a very large data set, with several interpretable conclusions and even more arguable ones. Among the most significant conclusions were (unsurprisingly) that the majority of cultures sampled unanimously perceived aging to be generally negative. However, statistically outlying countries such as China, Russia, Malaysia, New Zealand, and India showed perceptions of aging that were at-least neutral, and at times positive. Whereas respondents representing countries such as Serbia, Czech Republic, United Kingdom, and Argentina illustrated the most negative perceptions of aging overall. (Lockenhoff et al, 2009).

As for culturally consistent perceptions of age-related associates, items such as attractiveness, efficacy in daily activities, consistently decreased with age across all cultures. Contrastingly, culture-level associates such as knowledge, wisdom and societal respect virtually all saw consistent gains, across all cultures, as age increased (Lockenhoff et al, 2009).

Interpretations of this information (not excluding the vast amount of data not mentioned here) could take-form in a variety of ways. The author's interpretation was relatively succinct; cross-cultural consensus of aging trajectories across age-related and culture-level associates holds implications for how aging perceptions are shared across cultures. (Lockenhoff et al, 2009). Measures that illustrate dimensions of cognitive ability and physical functioning show relatively unanimous decline across cultures (McArdle, Ferrer-Caja, Hamagami, & Woodcock as cited by Lockenhoff et al, 2009), while measures of concrete intelligence such as social/emotional reasoning and overall well-being are, at least, fairly inert across cultures (Mcardle etal, Charles & Carstensen, as cited by Lockenhoff et al, 2009). The authors of this particular study conclude that the results for culture-level perceptions are relatively reliable as a descriptor of perceptions of aging across cultures - though, there is still more work to be done to refine and interpret outcomes for age-related associates.

What inferences are we to draw from the literature presented and it's authors' conclusions? This question is quasi-philosophical; a succinct answer will not be found in a dataset, publication, or resource. At best, one might be able to expand upon what we already know; culture and ethnicity have discrete, consequent outcomes for aging perceptions. But is this conclusion entirely generalizable to perceptions of aging that, at this moment, are unanimous between cultures?

The quasi-philosopher may attempt to categorize this phenomenon under the umbrella of 'human-nature' - certain outcomes should be expected across populations, but so too should exceptions. The quasi-sociologist might examine how patterns of governance, historical trajectories and gross domestic product influence these patterns of age-related and culture-level associations within different cultures and across various geographies.

Ultimately, the lens one examines this information through will allow for extrapolation in a variety of esoteric directions. Hence, it may not be all that productive to trace causation of the phenomenon we see here. Instead, remaining mindful of the time and place in which this data is produced, and deriving the mere essence of the conclusion will help in accepting what is presented - patterns of consistency, inconsistency, and a phenomenon that is wholly and inexplicably human in nature as it relates to aging and subjective interpretation.

Chapter 4
Socioeconomic Factors

"What person of a certain age doesn't hanker for smoother, plumper, more youthful-looking skin? The surgeon's knife is no longer the only option. More people are getting 'lifts' by nipping into cosmetic clinics that offer quick, non-surgical procedures. You can do it in your lunchtime."

- Timmermans and Berg

Introduction

Age has its own economy. Whether by virtue of pursuing a fountain of youth, such as through purchase of age-reversal pharmaceuticals, or buying age-appropriate infotainment (see; netflix kids), age, aging, and anti-aging are economic conduits to product-hungry consumers - eager to achieve comfort, satisfaction, and self-placation by increasingly grandiose economic means. 'Product-hungry' may be a brash misnomer to describe the state of age-focused consumers - it is more useful to describe consumers' marketplace behaviours through the lens of age-related ideals. Separate from this commercial-sphere, there is also a public-sector economy of age, which has its own socio-economic ripple-effects through governmental budgets and expenditures across the globe.

It goes without saying that marketing is not necessarily a game of 'best-product takes-all'. If this were the case, the market for age-reversal products would surely collapse. This is to say that many for-profit enterprises operating in this market-space are not regulated by governmental bodies such as the FDA and Health Canada, ultimately leaving their product-marketing claims unchecked, which leads to an inevitable inflation of product efficacy claims. Regardless, selling an intangible ideal like 'youthfulness' does not necessarily require tangibly effective products. Determination of product-efficacy, in this case, is most-often a by-product of affective state-change within consumers after product-purchase. That is to say, if there is an affective change in a given consumer's outlook, attitude, or self-perception by virtue of purchasing a product, the product has done its job - delivering relief, comfort, or placation to the internal burdens of a consumer's psyche, regardless of the product's measurable ability to delivering on it's marketing claims and intended tangible effects.

Alan Petersen is a Sociologist working with Monash University in Australia. Much of his research focuses on how markets capitalize on anxieties surrounding aging. In his 2018 paper 'Capitalising on ageing anxieties: Promissory discourse and the creation of an anti-ageing treatment market' Petersen illuminates a noteworthy paradox; Aging, despite having diffuse and impactful economic consequences, is pregnant with potential for spurring free-market competition. Suffice to say, despite burdening a society's fiscal infrastructure with higher costs associated with health and social accommodations, there is significant money to be made by private-sector entrepreneurs specializing in age-reversal merchandising, procedures, and philosophy (Petersen, 2018).

Sociology happens to be ripe with researchers focused on why patterns of negative-attitude tend to form around the idea of growing older. There is well-documented support for a theory of anti-aging culture being tethered to aspects of pseudo-biological sciences - often twisted and misrepresented to further stoke the flame of age-anxiety. There are notable social consequences of this phenomenon, mainly the covert fortification of ageism in a given society. We will discuss these and other social impacts in finer detail later in this chapter.

Biological science itself does not necessarily condemn aging by casting it in a connotatively aversive light. However, marketing strategies of anti-aging therapy, or AAT companies are aggressive purveyors of ageist motives, often portraying older age (or, at the very-least, loss of youthful vitality), as an undesirable defect of the human condition. One that can be remedied, in-whole or in-part, by pharmaceutical or biomedical means. (Vincent et al, 2008).

Many sociologists observe that when the notion of 'age' is exclusively understood as a biological process, societal and sociocultural issues surrounding age are often obscured. Of course, these effects take-form in a variety of ways across different cultures according to unique cultural values and age-related perceptions. For example, it has been observed that when aging is illustrated to exclusively mean 'biological aging', societal measures of healthy aging, respect for the elderly and acquisition of knowledge throughout the lifespan become distorted and undermined. Simply put; our understanding of age through a sociocultural lens begins to break-down when society adopts an exclusive, biologically centric, perception of age and aging (Vincent et al, 2008).

A salient question remains; what is it about biological aging that unleashes such ravenous anxiety and pandemonium in predominantly capitalist societies? Theories that attempt to answer this question are largely focused on attributional consequence; "I can attribute this newly acquired detriment to getting older, and as a result of getting older, many bad things could happen".

To extrapolate, sociologists sometimes see social and economic trends arise by virtue of people carrying a heavy conscience - guilt about specific aspects of the 'self' that are believed to require amelioration. The most salient theory that attempts to explain age-anxiety illustrates a link between growing old and the aforementioned notions of guilt and attributional consequence. Specifically, people belonging to north-american nationalities carry significant stress about becoming 'burdensome' as they progress into old-age; effectively burdening society, the healthcare system, and their families with issues that are expensive and time-consuming. Part of this anxiety relies on a widely-held assumption that accommodating by-products of aging may require intensive involvement by a support-network of many individuals. This fear of becoming a burden moulds engagement-patterns between individuals in a society and AAT providers, giving rise to a great-deal of socioeconomic activity in for-profit marketplaces, social-domains, public infrastructure, and beyond. This is the penultimatum of the prevailing theory for age-related anxiety; fear creates drastic cultural change - this has the potential to modulate many foundational aspects of a given society (Cardona, 2007, 2008).

Before further exploring this analysis, it is important to mention that anti-aging therapy is not synonymous with gerontology. AAT refers specifically to businesses or practices that market themselves with definitive intent to treat analogues of aging that carry cultural significance. This definition does not exclude medicinal practitioners as a whole - it is not uncommon for dermatologists to treat patients who are looking to restore elasticity to their skin in the hopes of looking more youthful. Gerontology, on the other hand, explores and treats categorical medical illnesses that are, or may be, associated with aging. I suppose one could make clear cut distinctions between AAT's and Gerontology by employing a diagnostic manual such as the ICD (international classification of diseases). AAT's are less-likely to interact with consumers looking to remedy ICD diagnosis', whereas gerontologists are far more likely to interact with this clientele. That is not to say that AAT's do not have a well-founded foothold in medicine - they do. In fact, the United States commissioned the American Academy of Anti-Aging Medicine, also known as A4M, to create interdisciplinary pathways to anti-aging treatment. Anti-aging consumers in the United States are afforded greater peace of mind knowing that their treatments and practitioners must earn the approval of a medically rigorous regulatory body. However, blending of AAT's with prestigious medical designations has not been easy, ultimately creating political and professional discord that continues to strain relationships between AAT's, healthcare providers, and medical designates (Katz, 2001, 2002). This distinction is important to remember as we approach this topic from different directions.

AAT's constitute enormous transnational enterprises. The industry itself is expected to exceed $216 billion US in 2021, and is projected to grow compoundingly by 7.5% every year thereafter. The rise of this omnipresent industry is grassroots in origin, despite still existing in relative infancy when compared to other commonplace industries.

Petersen and Krisjansen (2015) assert that the unprecedented market evolution of AAT's really took-off in the 1990's. This was a time of exciting development in biotechnology and bioscience - most notably occuring in the wake of accomplishments made by the human genome project. This groundbreaking research project eclipsed much of the other scientific discourse and discovery of the time, effectively 'stealing the floor' by captivating the world with future-like progress and innovation in biological and life-sciences. The idea that society was nearing a 'great-leap' in evolutionary potential was imbued to the masses with utilization of metaphors such as "genetics hold the key" superimposing media narratives and headlines. Needless to say, society expected a biotechnical revolution to occur with the incoming turn of the century - the turn of the century did not disappoint in this regard.

Financial investment by sole-proprietors, corporations, and governments skyrocketed in biosciences research and development with the promise of revolutionary strides in understanding the human life-cycle and positively upending the way we live. Foresight into complex and partially understood medical mysteries was an attractive concept, flaunting significant potential to save money in both public and private economic sectors.

Population aging, previously seen as an economically catastrophic problem, became fertile ground for profit generation and cutting age-related expenditures. Slogans such as "productive aging" began to perforate governmental and private-sector discourse surrounding the dilemma of aging. There were finally justifiable grounds by which people could be encouraged to remain productive and self-reliant as they progressed through their lifetime - for better and for worse. AAT providers quickly capitalized on the opportunity to unleash the powerful and popular strides made by science on the 'baby-boomers'. They represented a promising demography were considered to be healthy, affluent, and anxious about aging (Petersen, 2015).

It is no longer the 1990's - as evidenced by the inexorable evolution of the anti aging industry from then to now. Treatments and products are now inextricably diverse - seeing the rise of entirely novel classifications of products and supplements. There is now a vast illusion of choice for consumers looking to ameliorate their aging anxieties, such as; nutraceuticals (anti-aging foods), cosmeceuticals (cosmetic treatments), regenerative therapies, stem-cell therapies, chemical peels, dermal fillers, the list is truly non-exhaustive. Surgical proprietors have also refined their treatments and techniques in recent years, leading to enhanced access to cosmetic procedures such as 'tummy-tucks', breast augmentation, and botox with previously unthinkable speed, ease, and affordability. Contemporary approaches to marketing and health-sciences have also blurred the lines that previously classified AAT's as discrete interventions with exclusive purpose - it is no-longer uncommon to hear of a treatment that is colloquially understood to fend-off aging, yet indicated to fulfill a different purpose. Breast augmentation and anti-cellulite treatments are excellent examples - these procedures are often marketed in unique ways to avoid being associated with connotations that follow AAT's, yet are most-often employed in an anti-aging capacity (Petersen, 2015).

It goes without saying that the adoption of AAT's by corporations that would become hugely wealthy and influential throughout the 1990's and 2000's have influenced societal notions of, and philosophical relationship with aging. These days, we see individualism prevail in our consumer-centric capitalistic culture. Elevation of the self, whether by means of material wealth, appearance, or self image is a prevailing motivator for society, in rabid and perpetual pursuit of purpose, meaning, and gratification in life. Removal of barriers such as cost, wait-time, risk, and availability have facilitated the growth of a mammoth industry that compounds 7.5% growth annually, and is nearly unavoidable in all dimensions of public-life. Widely-adopted notions of age as a genetic detriment has also fortified the rise of this industry, the roots of which happened to propagate coincidentally with an exponential leap in biological science and genetic engineering during the 1990's. We now see that consumer-fear is the fuel that continues to drive this industry toward even greater profits and influence within societies across the globe. This fear is rooted in the belief that one's age could be detrimental to the prosperity of others - a notion that remains deeply contested throughout the literature.

Chapter 5
Current Anti-Ageing Medicine and Technology

"Do not go gentle into that good night but rage, rage against the dying of the light."

- Dylan Thomas

Introduction

Aging is the mother of all diseases. It is the primary cause of blindness, deafness, immunodeficiency, cancer, frailty, diabetes, heart disease, neurodegeneration, disability, suffering, and death (Jaul & Barron, 2017). Aging is the most malignant and serious of all bodily afflictions because it has no cure and a mortality rate of 100%. The physiological processes of ageing are inseparable from globally-recognised diseases, such as cancer and strokes, which kill hundreds of thousands of individuals every day. However, just because aged decline and death has been and continues to be inevitable and universal, does not mean we should be unconcerned or complacent in finding a way to address it. Medicine exists to enable individuals to live healthy and fulfilling lives. Individuals working on the frontiers of medical research, then, must focus not only on treating individuals in aged decline but on stopping the greatest producer of death and disease: ageing itself. The holy grail of medicine is to cure age-related disease and degradation— humanity's prime source of sickness. In recent years, scientists have made real progress toward this goal. There has been an explosion of scientists and entrepreneurs bringing to market products, services, and data related to slowing or curing ageing. The purpose of this chapter is two-fold. It will begin by describing ageing as a disease. It will then discuss the myriad of ways individuals can and do attempt to extend their longevity by combating the hallmarks of aging. In particular, this chapter will focus on two classes of activity that result in longevity extension: activating innate human biological pathways to induce anti-ageing, and clinically intervening to reverse the effects of ageing.

Ageing as a Concept

It would be inappropriate to begin several chapters discussing methods and technologies for longevity enhancement without briefly describing the processes of aged decline. Researchers only recently mapped the physiological processes that cause age-related degeneration and disease. In 2013, a landmark paper identified the hallmarks of aging as genomic instability (producing dysfunctional cells), telomere attrition (preventing the repair of DNA and causing cellular damage), epigenetic alterations (the build-up of certain cellular markers of ageing), loss of proteostasis (causing misfolded proteins), deregulated nutrient-sensing (causing impaired insulin sensitivity), mitochondrial dysfunction (causing cell death and low energy), cellular senescence (causing persistent inflammation), stem cell exhaustion (preventing tissue regeneration), and altered intercellular communication (impairing immune and cellular responses) (López-Otín et al., 2013). For the first time, there is now wide agreement in the age-studying community concerning the biological dimensions of ageing. But how is ageing measured scientifically? If we are to accept that it is possible to extend human longevity, then ageing as a biological process must be distinguished from growing older in time. It is theoretically possible to become older in time without becoming older physiologically. Like the identification of the hallmarks of ageing, the science of measuring ageing is brand-new and exciting. There are two important concepts when it comes to measuring ageing. First, chronological age as in the number of years since an individual was born. Second, biological age as in the measure of the youth of the cells of an individual. It was only in 2018 that precise biological age measurement was made possible by the creation of the epigenetic clock theory of ageing which uses DNA methylation-based biomarkers and large datasets to track aging (Horvath & Raj, 2018). In brief, cells build-up methyls on a molecular level as they maintain themselves over time. These methyls can be measured and function better than any other indicator as a marker of biological ageing. Researchers, therefore, can use large clinical data-sets to assess individuals' methylation profiles and predict when death will occur (Colicino et al., 2020). Despite the fact that the science of measuring and analysing longevity is still in its beginning stages, there is a great body of evidence concerning interventions that enhance one's longevity to which we will now turn.

Interventions Against Ageing

Perhaps the simplest and most well-established method for living longer is caloric restriction. In virtually every living organism extant on Earth, caloric restriction extends longevity. The metabolism of an organism's cells defines its ageing processes. Caloric restriction, also known as dietary restriction, is a process in which an organism substantially reduces its food/caloric intake but stops short of entering a state of malnutrition. Studies have shown that caloric restriction extends the average and maximum lifespans of yeast, flies, worms, fish, rodents and rhesus monkeys

(Fontana, 2010). The results can be dramatic, such as a threefold increase in lifespan for worms and a 30-50% increase in mice (Fontana et al., 2011). In rodents and monkeys, lab animals predictive of human physiology, caloric restriction not only enhanced life-span but reduced age-related loss of function and disease incidence (Anderson et al., 2009). In humans, studies have found that caloric restriction reduces markers of diabetes, cardiovascular disease, and cancer (Fontana, 2010). In terms of human life-expectancy enhancement, one study extrapolated animal data to conclude that moderate long-term caloric restriction (a 20% reduction in standard caloric intake at 25 years of age) would have enabled Albert Einstein to have lived an extra 5 years (dying at the age of 81 instead of 76) (Redman p. 284, 2011). But how many fewer calories does caloric restriction require to bring about longevity enhancement? Most estimates for a regular diet recommend a 2,500 daily calorie intake for men. If implementing a standard caloric restriction of 25% (meaning 75% standard recommended caloric intake), the calorically restricted intake for a man would be 1875 calories. For context, the standard recipe for a McDonald's Big Mac has 570 calories. To summarise, caloric restriction serves to "elevate resistance to oxidative stress, reduce macromolecular damage, and increase lifespan in model organisms" (Fontana, 2010). Caloric restriction is a proven method for longevity enhancement.

However, readers may simply think about feeling hungry to understand the undesirability of living in a chronic state of caloric restriction, even if it is longevity enhancing. Thankfully, there are several ways to achieve the benefits of caloric restriction without dealing with unpleasant side effects. One method for producing this effect is adopting a diet centered on the practice of intermittent or periodic fasting. Fasting has biological impacts similar to dietary restriction. These dietary interventions have the effect of enabling "cell protection and repair as well as the clearance of damaged cells and intracellular components, in part through the modulation of conserved stress-response or nutrient-sensing pathways" (Longo et al., 2021, p.27). In order to trigger this effect, intermittent fasting requires not eating for 12 to 48 hours repeated every 1 to 7 days and periodic fasting requires not eating for 2 to 7 days repeated once a month (47). As a result of following one of these protocols, studies suggest that one could significantly lower risk of aging and its ailments including heart disease, neurodegeneration, diabetes, and cancer (56). For individuals uninterested in fasting, time-restricted eating may be an option for extending one's longevity. Studies on mice have shown that eating a single meal a day, (as opposed to snacking throughout the day) delays the onset of age-related disease and extended lifespan (Chaix et al., 2014). Fasting and time-restricted eating are excellent alternatives for longevity-enhancement when compared to the extreme of caloric restriction.

The problem, however, is that all these forms of dieting are not easy to implement and take exceptional commitment. What options exist for leveraging the benefits of caloric restriction for individuals who want to consume as many calories as they want whenever they want? The answer is that it is possible to use pharmaceuticals to trick one's cells into behaving as if they were in caloric deficit. Drugs such as metformin, rapamycin, and acarbose (often used in the treatment of diabetes) have been the focus of research and interest given their longevity-promoting effects and strong safety track-records. Metformin is the most famous and popular of these drugs. A recent study showed that metformin results in the attenuation of the aforementioned hallmarks of ageing in that it improves metabolic function and cellular communication, suppresses inflammation, exhibits protective effects against the cancer-causing genetic damage that accumulates in life, improves mitochondrial effectivity, reduces pathways causing stem-cell exhaustion, regulates epigenetic ageing, prevents telomere attrition, and suppresses cellular senescence (Kulkarni et al., 2020). Moreover, a study published in 2019 had 51 to 65-year-old men take metformin, a steroid, and human growth hormone for one year and, as a result, showed a 2-year decrease in biological versus chronological age (Fahy et al., 2019). Another drug of recent interest is rapamycin. Studies have shown that rapamycin increases lifespan in mice, prevents age-related disease in animals and humans, and prevents the onset of cellular senescence (Blagosklonny, 2017, p. 35493). Interestingly, rapamycin reduces the appearance of ageing on a clinical and molecular level when applied as a cosmetic product on the skin (Chung et al., 2019). The last drug of interest is acarbose which a study showed to have improved health and lifespan in aging mice by reducing the severity of post-meal glucose spikes (Harrison et al., 2019). Overall, research indicates that fasting-mimicking drugs can act as alternatives or compliments to caloric restriction and fasting.

All of the options discussed thus far bring about longevity enhancement through changing human cellular metabolism. Like the beneficial effects of caloric restriction, there are other means by which applying 'stress' to cells produces longevity-enhancing effects. Exercise is an example of an activity where 'stressing' the human body enhances its longevity. High intensity interval training and endurance training are effective means to enhance telomerase activity and telomere length and thereby reduce cellular senescence and improve cellular regenerative capacity (Werner et al., 2019). Moreover, aerobic exercise like running can improve one's cognition and IQ, and prevent neurological decline in ageing (Colcombe et al., 2004). While gaining muscle does not extend longevity on a cellular level, frailty in old age increases one's risk of death and injury and can be mitigated with resistance training. Another variety of physical stresses that can be applied to the body for anti-ageing effects are changes in temperature. Individuals that bath in saunas between 4 and 7 times per week at a temperature of 78 celsius may have a "50% lower risk for fatal heart disease, 60% lower risk for sudden cardiac death, 51% lower risk for stroke, 46% lower risk for hypertension' and a 40% lower risk for all cause mortality" (Patrick, 2019). The mechanism behind these benefits is that heat stress activates genes that express heat shock proteins that work to ensure the integrity and function of proteins. This is why a study showed that heat stress, also known as hyperthermic conditioning, introduced a genetic mutation which produced a 65% enhancement in the lifespan of nematode worms (Lithgow et al., 1995). The cold, too, might be useful in enhancing one's longevity. Cold therapy may fight persistent inflammation (indicative of ageing resulting from the build-up of senescent cells) and increase the synthesis of dendrites thus having nero-protective effects (Patrick, 2016). Altitude and air composition also contribute to longevity. A study showed that hyperbaric oxygen therapy (being in an environment with 100% oxygen and higher atmospheric pressure) increases telomere length and the clearance of senescent cells in human trials by producing the regenerative effects that normally come with hypoxia (Hachmo et al., 2020). Researchers have also investigated the potential for longevity extending effects of stressors including oxidative stress, ionizing radiation, and other synthetic/natural compounds (Kahn, 2010). Yet not all forms of stressing the body result in anti-ageing. Chronic psychological stress is associated with tumour development and suppression of natural killer cells which are important to effective immune protection (Salleh, 2008). Similarly, there is no benefit to the physiological stress of smoking and it causes cancer and cardiovascular diseases. Like anything, there are limits to the amount of biological 'stress' that is beneficial. Exercise can cause injury, saunaing can cause heatstroke, cold exposure can cause hypothermia, and so on. Nevertheless, the evidence is clear that longevity enhancement can result from activating anti-ageing pathways by causing stresses to the human body's biological processes.

The last area of interest in regard to activating innate human longevity pathways and preventing ageing is eating the right types of foods and nutrient compounds. Moderating the number of calories one consumes alone is not sufficient to achieve optional longevity benefits. The best possible diet for longevity as established by research is the Mediterranean diet. This diet is defined as a "balanced combination of fruit and vegetables, fish, cereals, and polyunsaturated fats [eg. nuts and olive oil], with a reduced consumption of meat and dairy products and moderate intake of alcohol, primarily red wine" (Daniele et al, 2017). Readers will no doubt have heard that they should avoid the overconsumption of sugar, processed foods, meat, and alcohol if they want to live healthfully, let alone achieve an enhancement in longevity. The reason for this advice is that processed food, highly sugared food, and high protein diets are difficult for individuals' digestive systems to process without causing cellular ageing. The types of foods in today's modern standard Western diet often have nutrient profiles that would never be found in the natural environment in which the human digestive system evolved over time. Readers may question, however, the reason for the Mediterranean diet's endorsement of alcohol in the form of red wine. To be clear, alcohol consumption is unhealthy and the safest amount of alcohol consumption is none (GBD, 2018). The reason red wine is recommended as part of the longevity-enhancing Mediterranean diet is that it is an excellent source of a special antioxidant called resveratrol that forms in grapes.

Resveratrol (and its related compound pterostilbene forming in blueberries) have been the object of considerable study in relation to its anti-ageing effects. These compounds show promise in improving the body's "antioxidant defence, regulation of the cell cycle, mitochondrial energy production, vascular tone, oncogene suppression, and many other phenomena" (Marcus & Morris, 2008). The reason behind the apparent well-functioning of resveratrol in preventing the onset of age-related disease is that it activates proteins called sirtuins.

The activation of sirtuins and their relationship to a naturally-produced compound called NAD+ (a coenzyme essential to maintaining cellular life and power) is exceptionally important in the context of ageing. In fact, one of the world's leading anti-ageing researchers has suggested that the "loss of NAD as we age, and the resulting decline in sirtuin activity, is thought to be the primary reason our bodies develop diseases when we are old but not when we are young." (Sinclair, 2019, p. 43). There are seven types of sirtuins that each serve vital functions in preventing ageing. They work to repair cellular damage and prevent senescence by removing the build-up of cellular plaques called acetyls (Grabowska et al,. 2017). The decline of sirtuin activity causes declines in NAD+ levels which, in turn, bring about age-related disease. In particular, the decline of sirtuin activity and NAD+ precipitates the "breakdown of the inter-tissue communication between the hypothalamus and adipose tissue, resulting in systemic functional decline over age and eventually limiting lifespan in mammals" (Imai & Guarente, 2017, p. 16017). Studies have shown that increasing NAD+ levels can improve cognition, prevent neurodegeneration, prevent age-related fattening, prevent age-related insulin insensitivity, increase muscle power, improve stem cell function, and improve liver health (Yoshino et al., 2018). The power of NAD+ cannot be overstated.

In fact, it is possible that over-supplementing NAD+ may cause the body to have too much power and drive tumor growth. How, then, does one increase their sirtuin activity and NAD+ levels. As mentioned in the paragraph before last, resveratrol and pterostilbene are natural supplements that aid in the maintenance of sirtuin activity. Curcumin is another natural supplement with potential for activating sirtuins, mitigating ageing inflammation, and extending lifespan in humans (Grabowska et al., 2017). In addition, there is an abundance of synthetic sirtuin-activating compounds that are being designed in laboratories for increased bioavailability (Bonkowski & Sinclair, 2016). Apart from promoting sirtuin activity, there are several methods for maintaining and increasing NAD+ levels in ageing. For instance, individuals may take supplements of precursor forms of NAD+. The company Elysium Health, backed by Five Nobel laureates, is among several companies offering a pill with a precursor called NR that is clinically proven to enhance NAD+ levels. The United States Special Operations Command announced in 2021 that it will start clinical trials of oral NAD+ supplements to improve soldier endurance and muscle power. Besides taking NAD+ pills, aAnother option is having NAD+ administered intravenously as it cannot be uptook directly by cells when eaten and requires a relatively inefficient process of chemical transformation in the body. Last, it is possible to stimulate an increased production of NAD+ through physical exercise. Research has established that both aerobic and resistance exercise training reverse age-dependent declines in NAD+ (Guia et al., 2019). The dosing and time to begin supplementing with resveratrol, curcumin, and NAD+ will vary based on the age and unique circumstances of an individual. In summary, it is essential to monitor and maintain sirtuin activity and NAD+ levels in order to achieve an extension in longevity.

So far we have discussed a variety of methods for achieving anti-ageing and longevity enhancement through innate biological pathways. These methods, even if taken together and performed diligently, can only enable modest increases in human longevity somewhere in the range of a few years to a decade. This is because ageing is multifaceted and so it is difficult for any one intervention to combat all hallmarks of ageing. For more robust longevity extension today, it is necessary to look to clinical interventions that go beyond leveraging one's existing biology. A large portion of the hallmarks of ageing are connected to cellular damage and repair. One promising anti-ageing intervention targeting cellular decay is to replace aged blood with young blood. Youthful blood has a variety of regenerative proteins and molecules which are less present in old blood (Pandika, 2019). More importantly, old blood has a build-up of harmful factors which speed up the ageing process that are less present in young blood (University of California, 2020). It appears that, ideally, one would have a blood composition that does not change in ageing such that the youthful factors do not decrease and the aged factors do not increase. There are several interventions that aim to fulfill this goal. Regular blood-plasma exchanges from young persons to old persons could be one option for longevity extension. Another option could be fixing the aged bone marrow that produces flawed blood cells. A study in 2020 showed that young bone marrow transplantation attenuates age-related cognitive decline in mice (Kang et al., 2020). Therefore, it is conceivable that one could use stem cells or transplantation to replace old bone marrow with new bone marrow capable of producing high-quality blood. The composition and quality of blood has direct and important impacts on ageing and longevity extension.

If by analogy we think of blood as the oil which enables the body to function smoothly, then we may think of organs as the component parts of the engine which enable it to run. Another intervention, then, may be repairing and replacing aged organ cells directly. One option is to swap out old and underperforming organs with new lab-grown updates. The problem, however, is that organs are challenging to manufacture in laboratory settings because of their complexity, density, and requirement to be fed nutrients efficiently. However, there has been exciting progress recently in using 3-D printing to produce human tissues with one study demonstrating that it is possible to print a small functioning part of a heart (Skylar-Scott et al., 2019). Another option for producing new organs is not 3-D printing but growing them using other animals via a process called interspecies formation. In this method, scientists use gene editing to produce transgenic animals (pigs and sheep that have human DNA) that can grow transplantable human tissues (Los Angeles et al., 2018). A final important way to correct cellular damage is to use stem cells, which function to replace old and dying cells. Stem cells can be applied in an extraordinary array of use cases. They are used in treating spinal injury, heart disease, diabetes, muscular disorders, bone degeneration, and dental problems, to name a few (Mahla, 2016). Therefore, there is a strong presumption that stem cells can be deployed to combat the hallmarks of ageing and prevent the onset of serious age-related disease if used proactively. Organ replacement and stem cell therapy are forms of regenerative medicine that hold enormous promise as interventions to extend human longevity.

The final type of anti-ageing intervention that will be discussed in this chapter is gene therapy. Genetics have great influence over longevity. There is a small but growing proportion of people who live to be more than one-hundred years old. Studies have looked to profile the genetic makeup of these long-lived individuals to identify their common longevity-enhancing genes (Zhang et al., 2020). The identification of different genes that both extend and shorten human longevity will enable the use of gene editing as an anti-ageing therapy. There are several animal precedents to the use of gene editing to combat ageing. Researchers in China were able to use gene editing to bring about healthier and 25% longer-lived mice through changes to a single gene (Wang et al., 2021). Another study at the Salk Institute demonstrated that gene editing could stop accelerated aging in mice caused by Hutchinson-Gilford progeria syndrome (Beyret et al., 2019). The CRISPR/Cas9 gene editing technology behind both of these studies was discovered in 2013. The science of gene therapy is still in its infancy. While it is currently possible to perform gene editing on adult humans with the aim of enhancing longevity, this is an unproven and potentially dangerous route to a longer and healthier life given that the editing process can cause collateral damage to other parts of the DNA. Moreover, it is massively expensive and technically complex as cells have to be extracted, edited, and replaced. Gene editing and gene therapy will become increasingly useful and powerful tools for anti-ageing interventions as more longevity-promoting and inhibiting genes are discovered.

The purpose of this chapter was two-fold. First, it described the hallmarks of ageing as a process of biological degradation. Second, it discussed the ways in which individuals might consider extending their longevity today in terms of activating innate biological pathways and undergoing clinical interventions. More specifically, this chapter identified several cutting-edge practices and technologies for anti-ageing including caloric restriction, intermittent/periodic fasting, time-restricted eating, fasting-mimicking drugs, physical exercise, cold/heat therapy, hyperbaric oxygen therapy, comsumption of a the Mediterranean diet, supplementation of sirtuin-activating compounds, NAD+ supplementation, blood-plasma exchanges, bone marrow transplantation, stem-cell therapy, organ replacement, and gene therapy. In the next chapter, we will turn to a discussion of advanced future technologies which could enable humans to live hundreds of years longer or perhaps even indefinitely.

Chapter 6
The Future of Anti-Ageing Medicine and Technology

"There is nothing in biology yet found that indicates the inevitability of death."

- Richard Feynman

Introduction

In the last few decades, ageing research has produced amazing results. Indeed, individuals alive today will live longer on average than ever before. And, moreover, people today have a non-zero chance of living to 200 or 300 years old, or even indefinitely, thanks to the miraculous pace of innovation and technology. It is common sense, however, that living longer with the ailments of aged decline is a curse, not a blessing. Let's be clear, then, about the nature of a cure for ageing. A cure for ageing must enable individuals to live in a perpetual state of health and youth. Curing the disease of ageing, therefore, can be defined as inventing a method for suspending or reversing the negative physiological effects that occur to organisms over time. In short, curing ageing may be defined as extending one's health span indefinitely. As fantastic as this sounds, there is no reason why a cure for ageing is not possible in principle.

Human lifespans have been steadily rising in modernity. The average life expectancy for men and women in Western societies was about 30 years old in 1400, forty-three in 1850, and has reached about eighty today (Arrison, 2011). Death and age-related decline seem to come later and later. In 2021, the maximum human lifespan is defined at around 125 years old. Demographic trends show no indication of an upper biological limit or that human lifespans will stop increasing (Weon & Je, 2007). Human bodies have no biological expiry date. They have parts that break down which, in theory, could all be corrected. Thankfully, anti-ageing research daily brings science-fiction nearer to science fact. The purpose of this chapter is to discuss four leading futuristic fields of technology that have the potential of enabling humans to live indefinitely: nanotechnology, neurotechnology, pharmacology, and regenerative cell biology. In particular, this chapter will look to describe these technologies in relation to ageing, discuss progress and problems associated with their development, and offer projections regarding their implementation and potential for success. In brief, this chapter discusses options for eliminating ageing and making death a choice, not an inevitability.

Nanotechnology

One potential candidate for curing ageing is nanotechnology. Nanotechnology is the practice of manipulating matter on a molecular scale. In relation to curing ageing, nanotechnology involves using small particles or devices on the scale of atoms and molecules to combat the previously discussed hallmarks of ageing. The smallness of these entities is astounding. For context, a sheet of paper is around 100,000 nanometers thick, DNA is about 2.5 nanometers thick, and one nanometer is about how far a human fingernail grows in one second. Nanoparticles and nanobots are not merely imagined products of science-fiction writers. They exist today. Nanoparticles are small particles which can be made of everything from basic materials like copper or gold to high-tech manufactured matter like quantum dots which serve as nano-sized semiconductors. Nanoparticles currently have clinical applications for improving the resolution of medical scans and helping to implement genetic changes on a cellular level (Murthy, 2007). They also have promising applications in anti-ageing therapeutics. One study found that silica nanoparticle therapy enhanced mouse bone density, bone volume and bone formation without any identifiable negative effects (Weitzmann et al., 2015). Other research has looked to investigate the widespread use of nanoparticles in cosmetics for fighting the appearance of ageing in regard to hair loss, wrinkling, and photo-ageing (Kaul et al., 2018). There are, however, concerns about the unregulated sale of nanoparticles in regards to potential health and environmental hazards posed by their use and production, particularly if inhaled (Kaul). As a side note to our discussion on cosmetic nanoparticles, it is important to recognize there are constant innovations in the science of consumer cosmetics and dermatology aimed at reversing the physical appearance of aging, such as surgery, red light therapy, and retinol. Overall, based on the function and application of nanoparticles to date, it seems implausible that they alone will be the key to curing ageing, but the evidence points in the direction that they will aid in human longevity extension.

Nanobots may be a stronger potential candidate for curing ageing. Nanobots are devices that can carry out very specific programmed functions. Medical nanobots have the capacity to process information, sense chemical agents, move, and disperse drugs or interact with cells. Fans of the Startrek franchise will be well-aware of the fictionalised medical applications of Borg nanoprobes. Similar to nanoparticles, nanobots exist today and have established health applications. However, they are not little metal machines powered by batteries. Perhaps the most promising area of research in age-stopping nanotechnology is the project of building "biomolecular machines that are both encoded by and built from DNA sequences" (Ramezani and Dietz, 2020, p. 2). This approach uses folded DNA to make origami nanostructures that can be directed intelligently and carry payloads such as a pharmaceutical to a targeted site. The elegance of this approach to designing nanobots is that rather than constructing new materials and devices, nature's existing materials can be repurposed for good. There is strong evidence that it works. One study used cue-responsive DNA origami robots transporting molecular payloads to kill cancer growth in cockroaches (Douglas et al., 2012). Another study in China showed that autonomous DNA robots can be programmed to transport drugs to kill tumours and prevent their growth in pigs and mice (Li et al., 2018). The concern with these types of treatments, however, is that the receptor-based targeting mechanism for the killing of tumor cells is not perfect and occasionally damages healthy cells as well. In order to get around this limitation, a newly proposed method is to control the targeting of nanobots toward the killing of cancer cells using infrared light (Di et al., 2020). Another issue is that nanobots can be targeted and killed by the human immune system if it misidentifies them as pathogens. To avoid this issue, a study showed that nanobots used to deliver targeted therapy to the brain can be camouflaged to avoid being targeted by the immune system (Chen et al., 2021). In the last several years, there has been exciting progress and established evidence for the clinical application of nanotechnology for curing ageing.

What is remarkable about the prospect of having nanotechnology sufficiently advanced to cure the hallmarks of ageing is that it does not stop at eradicating most disease as we know it forever.

Beyond curative nanotech, it seems likely that you could have nanobots that enable you to live in a constant state of optimised health. Nanobots could go beyond solving ageing and act like the world's greatest performance-enhancing drug, enabling people to be smarter, stronger, and happier. Nanobots could clean your blood, repair your skin, remove plaques from your teeth, prevent a stroke, increase your muscle mass, and so forth. Nanobots could enable almost superhuman health. Yet, there are limitations to this future of advanced and accessible nanotechnology. Nanotechnology requires very sophisticated instruments and knowledge to produce biomolecular programmed cells or devices. In order to have more advanced nanotechnology, we need to continue to have improvements in computer technology. If improvements in artificial intelligence (AI) and computing slowed or stayed the same, we may never realise this future. One area of hope for the accelerated development of anti-ageing nanotechnology is the potential for a so-called point of singularity. This idea of a singularity is well-known to technology enthusiasts as the point at which artificial intelligence becomes smarter than humans and the progress of innovation becomes exponential and uncontrollable. In the event of a singularity, superintelligent machines could quickly research on creating nanobots capable of reversing ageing on a total bodily scale. Another issue is that the manufacturing, deployment, and monitoring of nanotherapy is difficult and expensive. The medical and production skills involved in manipulating matter on a molecular basis are uncommon and in short supply. Nevertheless, there is promise of overcoming this problem. In 2003, it cost $1 billion to have the whole human genome sequenced for the first time. Today any consumer interested in having their whole genome sequenced can get a report back after paying 250 USD and waiting a few months. Likewise, the first cell phones and computers were exceptionally expensive and owned only by governments. Now, citizens of the world's poorest countries can afford quality consumer electronics. There is a strong presumption that the costs in creating and deploying nanotechnology to cure ageing would fall over time, even if only the richest people could afford these therapies at first. In the last few decades, the proof-of-principle for the use of longevity nanobots has been established. In the future, it may take only time to enable the computational and manufacturing advances to enable people to live forever.

Despite the great potential for treating age-related disease using nanotechnology, the nanobots and nanoparticles we know today are incapable of curing the myriad and complex expressions of ageing on a total bodily scale. So long as the pace of advancement we know today does not slow, we may not have to wait long for nanobots that can cure ageing. Ray Kurzweil, a futurist and director of engineering at Google, has a track record of accurate predictions and was featured in a 2011 edition of Time Magazine for his suggestion that humans will achieve immortality by 2045. The reason for Kurzweil's prediction of 2045 is that the improvement of technology progresses at an exponential rate (just imagine, for instance, the staggering advancements in cellular and personal computing in the last several years). Since 1965, the pace of technological advancement has been defined by the famous Moore's Law which states that computing power doubles every year. Now, the pace of artificial intelligence computing power appears to be moving at an even faster pace. A study from Stanford indicates a doubling of AI computing power every 3.5 months (Perrault et al., 2019). This pace of progress is hard to imagine but is easily captured in consumer products. In 1975 people were playing pong in black and white. Today, you can put on a virtual reality headset and load yourself into hyper-realistic interactive games and even multiplayer universes. Nanotechnology capable of curing ageing may be a mere 24 years away if Kurzweil is right. And, in any event, it seems very plausible that it will be created before any young person today dies from the diseases of ageing.

Neurotechnology

Neurotechnology is another possible area of science that could solve ageing. Scientists could use neurotechnology to create digital brains that behave like real organic brains. In turn, individuals could upload their minds to the Internet or computer servers and persist as digital artefacts free from the biological constraints of aging. The implications and possibilities associated with this technology will be addressed in greater detail in a few paragraphs. Before getting over-excited, we should assess whether neurotechnology is a viable method for curing ageing. In order to accept this, we must first accept several presumptions. First, we must accept that it is possible to scan the human brain at a detail sufficient to reproduce it accurately in digital form. Second, we must accept that there is sufficiently advanced computer software or code to animate the digital brain architecture once it is scanned. Third, we must accept that there is computer hardware capable of running the 'live' computerised brain. Let us now discuss these presumptions in greater detail and assess whether it is reasonable to accept them.

In terms of producing an accurate and detailed scan of the brain, digitising a human brain is squarely in the realm of possibility. Scientists published a paper in 2019 which demonstrated that they could map the complete neutral networks of nematode worms at a single point in time (Cook et al., 2019). To be sure, human neural networks are larger and infinitely more complex than those of nematode worms and the study did not show it was possible to emulate the worm brain inside a computer. Nevertheless, this study is a proof-of-concept that it is possible to scan and map neural networks. Another prominent group of neurobiologists are part of the Blue Brain Project which has been operating since 2005 with the goal of digitally reconstructing and simulating a complete mouse brain. Even just in the last three years, teams working at Blue Brain have published amazing work. For instance, they created an algorithm that can connect neurons in a mouse neocortex (Reimann et al., 2019). They also mapped every neuron and glial cell in a mouse brain and anticipate a complete model of the mouse brain will be ready by 2024 (Erö et al., 2018). Finally, they intend to demonstrate in a forthcoming publication the existence of methods for microcircuit creation that can be generalized to building a whole brain region. Research is progressing on the foundational neurobiology needed to enable human brain emulation. It looks likely that we will have a completely detailed scan of the brain in the next several years.

The challenge, however, is that the granularity of the scan we can achieve in the next decade may be insufficient. A static perfect map of the brain may not cut it when it comes to uploading one's mind. It is possible that quantum phenomena in the brain's micro tubules may be the answer to understanding consciousness in a brain (Hameroff & Penrose, 2014). This is the idea that the brain waves which provide for human consciousness originate from the vibrations of these brain tubes which control cell division, transport, and shape. If this is true, scanning the brain for the purpose of bringing it consciousness may be impossible. So far as we know, quantum states are impossible to track in a detailed manner due to their unique physical properties. Likewise, it is possible that an accurate brain scan needs to track brain particles at a molecular and genetic scale as the expression of many genes toggles between active and inactive at different times (Sandberg, 2013). It is not currently possible to monitor and scan all molecules in an organism in real time. Current scanning techniques use electron microscopy and so offer only still shots of the ever-changing system that is the brain. If it is the case that a quantum/molecular scan of the brain is needed to emulate consciousness, it may take longer than expected for neurotechnology to enable immorality. Before this is determined, we may wait and hope that a standard scan is sufficient.

Now to discuss the software that can bring life to a scanned brain architecture. When it comes to a living brain, consciousness comes about as a result of the interactions of all the small molecules and parts inside of it. The mystery and complexity of the brain arises in its operation and not merely its static structure. Another challenge for using neurotechnology to cure ageing is that it is difficult to have software that models the real-life behavior of cells, even if they are cataloged and understood perfectly at a molecular level. It is far beyond current software technology and computing power to model the stochastic (meaning unpredictable or random) behaviour of single molecules let alone all the molecules in a human brain and spinal cord. Yet there is hope for advancement here as well. Artificial intelligence is accelerating the ability for scientists to model organic matter. In 2020, the world's most advanced AI, Google Deepmind, was able to solve modeling the folding behavior of proteins that previously had been expensive, very time consuming in taking months or years, and sometimes not even possible (Callaway, 2020). Yet, even if we are prepared to accept that an AI could radically speed up our capacity to model the stochastic molecules in a perfectly scanned brain, challenges are abound. Brains and the consciousness they produce are not isolated systems. They exist in and are influenced by the state of the bodies of which they are a part. In turn, bodies exist in and are influenced by the environments of which they are a part. All this is to say that to solve ageing via mind uploading might mean having to first model brains, bodies, and environments in great detail. Therefore, neurotechnology may be a poor solution to solving ageing as it is reasonable to believe this is a more difficult task than some of the other options for curing ageing we will discuss. Still, it appears possible that in the future neurotechnology can solve ageing.

What of the hardware required to enable neurotechnology to solve ageing? We have already addressed the fact that computing speeds are rapidly increasing and that this progress cannot slow if neurotechnology will solve ageing. But what about the implantable medical hardware required to make mind uploading possible? The idea of the 'self' each of us possesses comes about as a result of the configuration of our brain and the sorts of electrical signals that are occurring at any given moment. If it is possible to control the operation of the brain to a high degree, it could be possible to bring about any type of consciousness one desires. Elon Musk's neuroscience company Neuralink stands at the forefront of consumer neurotechnology that might, in time, make this wild concept a reality. This brain implant could be the answer to enabling humans to upload their brains and live digitally. The stated goal of Neuralink is to connect different areas of the brain in new ways in order to "treat a wide range of neurological disorders, to restore sensory and movement function, and eventually to expand how we interact with each other, with the world, and with ourselves." (Neuralink). It is the goal of Neuralink to solve memory loss, hearing loss, blindness, paralysis, depression, insomnia, chronic pain, seizures, anxiety, addiction, strokes, and brain damage using a brain chip. However, the long term plan for Neuralink is to go much farther and, for instance, enable people to communicate without speech or signs.

In terms of its practical use, the team at Neuralink developed an innovative method of inserting a small chip into the skull with attached super thin wires which are placed into the brain by a robot surgeon causing minimal damage to existing tissue. These wires go into the cortex of the brain where most sensing activities are regulated but do not penetrate the deep brain. Neuralink is working to find a way to build a robust device that can sit in the human brain without breaking down over time. In theory, this device has the capability to read and write the neural activity of humans. This would make it capable of selecting emotions, altering sensation, and performing key brain operations. However, Musk has yet to establish these claims or provide evidence that Neuralink can cure diseases of ageing. As of writing, the Neuralink team has only shown that it is possible to implant the devices into pigs and monitor brain activity to predict the position of their limbs (Neuralink, 2020). Neuralink has not shown it is possible in pigs to sense specific thoughts and intentional states that would exist in humans. Neuralink is soon starting clinical trials with persons suffering from paralysis. If these and future trials are successful in curing previously incurable diseases, then we may be optimistic about the use of neurotechnology hardware to enhance longevity and perhaps enable immortality. Overall, clinical trials and more time is needed to establish the usability and potential impact of brain machine interfaces but Neuralink is revolutionizing the science in the field of implantable neurotechnology.

Finally, beyond solving ageing as a disease, let us take a moment to consider the radical possibilities that could be unleashed by the discovery of the kind of advanced neurotechnology thus far discussed. If mind-uploading and simulation was possible and worked harmoniously with brain-machine interfaces, then we can reasonably expect that it also functions for several other purposes. For instance, this type of brain machine interface could enable users to interact with technology by thinking. Everything from switching lights, to working, to playing video games could be accomplished merely by thinking instead of pressing buttons. Another possibility is that the brain machine interface could be used to draw information from the Internet directly into one's consciousness. Today, solving a math problem or recalling a fact requires the exercise of knowledge. But with an advanced brain machine interface, it is possible that information could be beamed directly and seamlessly into your consciousness as if you had always known an obscure probability or historical date. Furthermore, there is the possibility that a brain machine interface could record and replay sensations and memories. If this is true, then sharing memories and experiences through these inferences would also likely be possible.

Another startling possibility is that neurotechnology could be used to duplicate whole individuals. If there exists a method for perfectly scanning and simulating brains such that individuals can live in digital form, then there is a strong presumption that it is possible to create duplicates of this scanned individual. This would allow there to be a theoretically infinite number of Stephen Hawkings or Albert Einsteins, or whichever individual producing value in digital form after their bodies break down. Still further, it could be possible to download computer-based consciousness back into organic human brains. Once a digital brain is created, the architecture of this brain could be replicated in a clone body or potentially created through an advanced brain machine interface. This would enable individuals to transfer into younger (or even new) bodies when age-related physiological decline begins. It is clear, then, that the advent of advanced neurotechnology offers a very different future for humanity and has far-reaching impacts beyond solving ageing. In these respects, neurotechnology is unlike any other method for curing ageing.

Pharmacology

Pharmacology is the third field of science that could present a cure for solving aging. It is conceivable that you could have an array of drugs that fix or prevent age-related physiological degeneration. Aubrey de Grey, a leading figure in the anti-aging world, authored a hypothetical proposal for curing aging called Strategies for Engineered Negligible Senescence (SENS). His proposal involves preventing cell atrophy, cleaning plaques outside cells, cleaning built-up plaques inside cells, and killing cancerous cells (DeGrey, 2007). Several of these aims are best achieved through pharmacological interventions. Yet the SENS proposal to address ageing is speculative in that many of the disorders it discusses, like cancer, have no effective treatments now or as of 2007 when de Grey proposed it. Let us take a closer look at the kinds of problems drugs would have to target in order to cure ageing, namely senescent cells and cellular plaque.

One target for anti-ageing drugs is the build-up of senescent cells. Cells become senescent when they stop functioning properly, for example, as a result of DNA damage. The body shuts cells down to prevent them from becoming cancerous or otherwise problematic. Once turned off, senescent cells emit inflammatory signaling proteins called cytokines that indicate to the immune system that they need to be destroyed. The problem is that the immune system weakens in ageing and thus senescent cells build-up. As more of these cells build-up, the level of systematic persistent inflammation in the body increases to a toxic level. The downstream impact of this form of chronic inflammation is heart disease, cancer, diabetes, kidney disease, fatty liver disease, and autoimmune and neurodegenerative disorders (Furman et al., 2019).

There are two types of anti-ageing drugs that could reverse this form of cellular ageing. First are drugs that are senolytic, meaning they kill senescent cells. Second are drugs that are senomorphic, meaning they modify senescent cells such that they do not contribute to the diseases of ageing. Research into these areas of pharmacology has gained traction and is increasing at a truly exponential rate (Mkrtchyan et al., 2020, p. 11). Some of the leading senolytic drugs include pharmaceuticals like Dasatinib and Navitoclax and natural supplements like Quercetin and Fisetin. The range of age-related disorders treatable through the use of these senolytics in animal trials is remarkable. Indeed, the list of specific age-related disorders which are attenuated by senolytics like these is too long to discuss here but is available in a review done by the Mayo Clinic Centre for Ageing (Kirkland & Tchkonia, 2020, p. 9). In addition, there are several clinical trials underway to assess the effectiveness of senolytics in humans. It is sufficient for our purposes to say that senolytic drugs are exciting in relation to curing ageing because they extend healthspan in animal trials (Xu et al., 2018). There appears to be low risk that senolytic drugs could damage healthy cells. We may expect in the next several years there to be a significant amount of clinical trial research published in which the human safety profile of senolytics will be determined. On the whole, drug-based senotherapy appears to be a very promising future drug for curing ageing.

Another area for pharmacology to combat ageing is to prevent the formation of heart and brain plaque. In order to achieve this aim, DeGrey proposes the discovery of advanced glycation end product (AGE) breaking drugs. These so-called end products are proteins that are found in people who are overweight and diabetic. They form in the body naturally but are found in high amounts in foods cooked in dry heat, like grilled red meat, which are common in modern diets (Uribarri et al., 2013). The concern with these types of proteins is that they cause cell dysfunction and lead to the expression of genes causing heart and brain disease. In particular, they lead to the stiffening, thickening, and calcification of blood vessels by increasing blood fat levels and causing inflammation (Nenna et al., 2015). There is also evidence that these end products contribute to brain dysfunction and death and speed up the progression of neurodegeneration, including Alzheimer's. AGEs interfere with the brain's cells ability to communicate with each other and cause oxidative damage to cells (Kikuchi et al., 2003). In recent years, there have been the discovery and testing of drugs to fight AGEs, notably statins, alagebrium and thiazolidinediones (Nenna). Besides AGEs, the brain builds up proteins called beta amyloid plaques. Exactly like AGEs these plaques kill brain cells by preventing intracellular communication and inducing oxidative stress (Kadowaki et al., 2005). It seems clear, then, that drugs that prevent the formation or enable the destruction of plaques in important body systems may be key to achieving a pharmacological cure to ageing. However, more time is needed to both discover and test these therapeutics. None of the drugs discovered to-date used in the treatment of heart and brain disorders cure these diseases.

Despite the widespread effective use of pharmacological interventions today, drugs have some inherent limitations in their ability to cure ageing. For one thing, drugs generally have temporary effects. Molecules that have biological effects degrade in the body over time. The stimulating effects of a cup of coffee, for example, do not last long. The consequence of the time-limited effectiveness of drugs is that any useful drug-based therapy against ageing may require very regular dosages. If this is true and anti-ageing drugs must be consumed regularly, there are two further problems with which to contend. First, the regular dosing of age-solving drugs may remain out of reach for virtually everyone for the foreseeable future if they are expensive to produce because of their raw materials or patents. Second, anti-ageing drugs may become less effective or require increasingly large doses to maintain effectiveness as a result of drug tolerance. Just as long-time coffee drinkers may need to reach for more cups per day to stay sharp, so may users of anti-ageing drugs require greater and greater numbers of pills to stay biologically young. Moreover, there is a problem in that the assortment of drugs needed to cure ageing would likely be numerous and have some overlap in terms of the biological pathways they regulate and activate. Because of this overlap, individuals taking anti-ageing drugs may develop cross-tolerance. For illustration, individuals who regularly consume nicotine have a higher alcohol tolerance even if they do not drink because both of these drugs act in some of the same internal pathways. This same problem could occur in regard to anti-ageing drugs.

A final substantial problem in the use of drugs to solve ageing is the potential for negative side effects. A famous adage is that there is no such thing as a free lunch. This is true in pharmacology as it is elsewhere. Drugs are imprecise and almost never achieve a single aim and a single aim only (eg. curing a headache without causing another potentially adverse biological response). There are risky side-effects possible in the consumption of even well-established drugs that are considered sufficiently safe to sell on supermarket shelves. Popular non-steroidal anti-inflammatory drugs like ibuprofen cause intestinal bleeding and death in thousands of cases every year (Mokhtare et al., 2013). If anti-ageing drugs are numerous and require regular dosing, the side effects may render them an unrealistic or unpleasant option for indefinite life extension. For these reasons, a pharmacological cure for ageing has serious challenges to overcome. Drugs may better work as supplementary interventions to other anti-ageing regimes than stand-alone cures for all forms of aged decline itself.

Overall, there is strong evidence for the use of drugs in treating ageing as a disease. Indeed, pharmaceutical companies and start ups are keenly interested in developing the sorts of drugs addressed in de Grey's SENS proposal. There are many research organisations dedicated solely to solving problems related to aging that have been backed by billionaires and companies like Google. These include Unity Biotechnology having made advancements in senolytics and anti-ageing antibodies, Calico Labs publishing on the mechanisms of ageing and why naked mole-rats do not have greater risk of death as they age, BioAge publishing on muscle and immune anti-ageing pathways, as well as AgeX, Juvenescence, and Athersys. There are also investor-backed venture capital funds which support anti-aging projects such as the Longevity Fund and the Methuselah Fund. We may have great hope, then, in a future where there exists a range of anti-ageing drugs that enable radical life extension. Whether these drugs will, however, offer a complete solution to ageing remains to be seen. As discussed, pharmacological interventions to disease necessarily encounter issues involving dosage, cost, drug tolerance, and side-effects. The bottom line is that drugs may slow or stop aspects of aging, but more time is needed before they offer a complete or low-risk solution.

Regenerative Biology

The last and most promising of cures of aging is regenerative medicine and, in particular, cellular manipulation or reprogramming. This is the process of changing how cells behave and altering the foundational principles upon which they operate. To understand how this works, it is productive to look at how different types of animals live and die. In the natural world, there are a few asexually reproducing animals like hydras, sponges, corals, and jellyfish that appear to be biologically immortal (Petralia et al., 2014). Among these animals, the jellyfish Turritopsis dohrnii is a notable example. This jellyfish has the capacity to revert its cells to an earlier stage of their life cycle. It can reset its biological age from old to young. The underlying reason for this capacity is that DNA hardly degrades even as it ages. Genetic information remains intact whereas the epigenome (in terms of the ways cells work for example) falls apart over time. Thus, the Turritopsis dohrnii can cheat death by resetting its age and scientists can clone a youthful and healthy copy of an old animal using its aged and sick cells. The problem is, however, that large and complex animals live nowhere as long as jellyfish. The longest living vertebrate is the Greenland shark which has a predicted lifespan of 250-500 years old. Humans live nowhere as long as this shark. The purpose of this section of the chapter, then, is to discuss how it is possible to use science to leverage what we know about biologically immortal species to enable a cure for ageing in humans.

Dr. David Sinclair's laboratory at Harvard is leading the cure for aging using cellular manipulation. The reason behind the success of the Sinclair lab is that they have developed a novel and well-supported explanation for the origin of the hallmarks of ageing. Sinclair calls this the Information Theory of Aging. Let us take a moment to explore this theory. In human bodies, all cells have the same DNA. The reason there are different cells is because of the epigenome which controls what genes are expressed and what particular cells are produced. Sinclair's lab contends that aging's root cause is the "accumulation of epigenetic noise that disrupts gene expression patterns" in that genes forget their identity and fail to function properly consequently causing disease and eventually death (Lu et al., 2020, p. 124). The cause of this epigenetic noise comes from DNA damage in terms of chromosome breaks. These breaks can be caused by regular life-sustaining bodily operations, chemical compounds, the sun's rays, medical x-rays, or a host of other environmental stresses that are toxic to cells. The upshot of this epigenetic noise is that cells lose their pure and original functionality and composition. The evidence for this theory of ageing is presented in Sinclair's lab which has shown that it is possible to speed up and reverse aging by manipulating cell's exposures and responses to epigenetic noise. Sinclair's first project was to show in 2019 that inducing greater amounts of epigenetic noise accelerates ageing. His lab achieved this aim by showing that genetically modified mice which had to work to paste back together breaks in their DNA showed greatly accelerated ageing and epigenetic drift (Hayano et al., 2019). Sinclair's second project was to show that you could reverse the biological age of cells. In 2020, Sinclair's lab demonstrated that it had succeeded in reversing aging on a cellular level in mammals. They proved that it is possible, like in the case of the jellyfish, to "reset the aging clock and prevent cells from ever losing their identity and becoming senescent" (Sinclair, 2019, p. 167). The Information Theory of Aging is supported by the fact that the Sinclair Lab was able to accelerate as well as reverse ageing and cure age-related blindness in regenerating mouse optic nerves.

Sinclair's discovery is nothing short of astounding. There are three exceptional features to Sinclar's discovery that are worth discussing. First, Sinclair's treatment to induce a reversal in cellular ageing uses embryonic stem cells called Yamanaka factors that have the capacity to induce age-reversal in any human cell type. This means that the procedure devised by Sinclair's lab could theoretically be applied anywhere in the human body, including the brain and spinal cord. Therefore, cellular reprogramming appears to have potential for a total rejuvenation therapy. Second, the anti-ageing treatment is delivered virally and the age reversal process can be toggled on-and-off using antibiotics. This makes the process of treatment relatively painless and free of risk and side-effects. There is, however, some risk if the reversal process is not stopped at the right moment as going too far back in time turns cells into tumors. Third, there does not seem to be a limit for the number of times you can perform the cell age reversal therapy. It appears possible, in theory, to reverse ageing time and time again using the same process without risk or damage to cells. For example, it could be that an 80-year-old individual goes every week for cellular reprogramming therapy until they are biologically 20 but chronologically 80. It would be fantasy as reality to see your loved-ones ageing back in time each week to become more youthful. In future, more evidence will be available about the use and risks of cellular reprogramming as a means to solve ageing. This therapy will soon be explored in primate spinal cords and in human trials. As of now, it suffices to say that cellular reprogramming looks to be the single most effective and low risk solution to solving ageing as a disease.

The purpose of this chapter was to discuss how we might live forever. In particular, this chapter focused on assessing how and why the sciences of nanotechnology, neurotechnology, pharmacology, and regenerative cell biology could be the answer to curing ageing. In terms of ranking these potential pathways to curing ageing, regenerative cell biology is the most promising field of science. Its solution to ageing is the most elegant and scientifically well-established among these four pathways. It is unclear exactly in what order the other technologies would fall. Nanotechnology shows great promise for curing ageing and has proof-of-concept work complete. Similarly, while it is new and unproven, neurotechnology offers the most radical possibilities and greatest potential for significant improvement in the next several years. Finally, in terms of pharmacology, drugs can be used to treat ageing today but involve a host of problems inherent to their use and production. To conclude this chapter is to offer a word of advice: individuals interested in perpetual youth would do well to do everything in their power to stay alive as long as possible. The cure to ageing is coming. Based on current evidence, it would be irresponsible to dismiss the idea that you will stop ageing at some point in your lifetime. In the next chapter, we will turn to a speculative analysis of the economic effects of ending the disease of ageing.

Chapter 7
Economic Benefits to Anti-Ageing and Healthspan Extension

"The ultimate resource in economic development is people. It is people, not capital or raw materials that develop an economy."

- Peter Drucker

Introduction

Health and wealth go hand in hand. Curing or slowing the effects of biological ageing would bring about exceptional economic benefits and, in turn, improve individuals' quality of life. Welfare and living standards increase when people live longer and healthier because they are more productive and innovative. The synergistic effects of health and wealth can be dramatic. The fact is that modest extensions to life-expectancy have large impacts on economic prosperity. According to one economic study, "from 1970 to 2000, gains in life expectancy added about $3.2 trillion per year to [the United States] national wealth" and "gains in life expectancy over the century were worth over $1.2 million per person to the current population" (Murphy & Topel, 2006, p. 872). It is clear, then, that one can benefit when people living in society live longer and healthier lives. The purpose of this chapter is to discuss the economic benefits arising from suppressing or reversing the effects of ageing. In particular, it will look at the economics of ageing in the context of healthcare costs, old-age support costs, labour market productivity and participation, budgets and public expenditure, consumer behaviour, population growth, health equity, population growth, and resource consumption. Overall, this chapter serves to indicate that curing ageing will have massive positive economic benefits.

The most apparent economic benefit to curing ageing is that it would eliminate the high cost of treating ageing as a disease. Elderly individuals are high consumers of healthcare services compared to individuals in other age categories. One study analyised per capita health care spending by age group in the United States and wealthy comparator countries in 2015. It found that the mean per capita healthcare expenditure of individuals aged over 65 was 468% more than individuals aged 0-19 and 241% more than individuals aged 20-64 (Papanicolas et al., 2020). Persons suffering from the ailments of ageing are the greatest users of healthcare services and the considerable majority of healthcare expenditure in the developed world is focused on treating individuals suffering from the effects of old-age. Indeed, a significant portion of healthcare expenditure is allocated in treating people in the last few months of life. A study found that in the Canadian province of Ontario, approximately 10% of all healthcare expenditure was focused on the last year of a patient's life with costs spiking in the last 30 days of life (Tanuseputro et al., 2015). Given this information, it is clear there would be massive savings in reducing the the need to treat the elderly demographic. The simple reason why these savings would be substantial is that fighting against the current inevitability of age-caused death is highly expensive. A 2020 study looked at the economic burden of chronic age-related diseases in China, Japan, and South Korea. It projected for 2010-2030 that treating cardiovascular diseases, cancer, chronic respiratory diseases, diabetes, and mental health conditions, largely resulting from age, will cost $7.7 trillion in China, $3.5 trillion in Japan, and $1 trillion in South Korea (Bloom et al, 2020). Moreover, healthcare costs have a tendency to rise quickly. In the United States, healthcare costs for the elderly have steadily increased year after year since 1965 and increased at a rate of almost 15% per year between 1977 and 1984 (Waldo and Lazenby, 1984). Individuals and governments spend enormous resources treating serious age-related disorders only to prolong people's lives by a few months or years, often with minimal improvement to quality of life.

The problematic trend of increasing medical costs is compounded by the fact that there are increasingly large numbers of elderly persons accessing healthcare. The unusually large Boomer generation produced during a period of high birth rates, now 57-75 years old, is ageing and accessing healthcare services. This new and large aged population will produce massive increases on the cost of treating the diseases of ageing. In Canada, the number of individuals aged 85 and older will triple within 30 years (MacDonald and Hirdes, 2019). One study done by Canada's National Institute of Ageing found that long-term healthcare costs for the elderly are expected to increase from $22 billion to $71 billion annually within the next 30 years (MacDonald). This is the equivalent of healthcare expenditure increasing from 9% of personal income tax in 2019 to 19% of personal income tax by 2050 (MacDonald). The fact that treating age-related disease is becoming increasingly burdensome is problematic for two reasons. First, there are concerns about fairness. A small part of the payer population in publicly funded payer systems draw disproportionately on healthcare services. In Canada, individuals over the age of 65 represent about 16% of the total population yet represented 45% of healthcare costs in 2019 and are projected to represent 71% percent of the costs by 2040 (Globerman, 2021). Second, there are concerns about the quality of care. A cure for ageing as a disease would enable massive amounts of public funds to be diverted to more productive uses.

In terms of the level of health costs in North America as a share of gross domestic product, healthcare spending represented 17.7% of the United States GDP and 11.5% of the Canadian GDP (CMS, CIHI). This expenditure could be reallocated to more productive ends or returned to people in the form of lower taxes if an effective and affordable cure for ageing emerged. To summarise, it is becoming increasingly costly to treat the diseases of ageing and, moreover, there are an unprecedented number of people requiring these treatments. There are serious concerns about whether continuing the state-funded war against ageing is even economically feasible.

Apart from the primary and direct health costs, ageing is costly because of its secondary effects. For instance, age-related health shocks and physiological deterioration can lead to early retirement, whether through pension plans or government disability benefits (Jones et al., 2019). Early retirement is a largely negative economic phenomenon. One problem is that individuals may be claiming government benefits for longer than they otherwise would have provided that they maintained good health. But age-related early retirement is also problematic because individuals can reduce their earning power and potentially suppress their consumption and investment. What's more, exiting the labour market early is a wasteful use of individuals' human capital to produce economic value using education, training, and skills. While it could be argued that early retirees are good for the labour market in that they make room for new entrants, this does not appear true given that there is low substitutability between elderly and young workers (Matsukura et al., 2018). Retirement is a negative economic outcome because individuals produce less economic value themselves and reduce their spending. Retirement runs counter to increasing annual economic growth which depends on increasing the number of goods and services produced. Consumer spending is the strongest factor impacting GDP growth and contractions. Ageing has similar indirect costs even if individuals cannot or will not retire early. Individuals in poor health are less economically productive and earn lower wages than individuals who are healthy (Chirikos and Nestel, 1985). In short, ageing results in serious indirect economic costs in the form of decreased productivity, lower labour market participation, and suppressed economic engagement. These costs would be obviated to a significant degree by a cure for ageing, as previously discussed.

Aging is the world's leading cause of death and suffering. It is unsurprising, then, that another form of savings brought about by a cure for ageing would be lowering the cost of death. Certainly, people would still die in a world where ageing has a cure but it is patently clear that most people die from age-related illness. Indeed, one study analysing health data in World Bank income groups found that "35 million people will die in 2005 from heart disease, stroke, cancer, and other chronic diseases.", all of these being chronic age-related diseases (Strong et al, 2005, p. 1587). Diseases of ageing are negative economic drivers because they cause the foreclosure of otherwise earned income and economic activity. Chronic diseases of ageing have a cost in that dead individuals would have otherwise likely continued to be engaged in the economy and society. What's worse, the socioeconomic distribution of aging-related death and suffering is highly unequal. In reference to the 35 million dead in 2005, "20% of these deaths [occurred] in high-income countries—while 80% [occurred] in low-income and middle-income countries." (Strong et al., 2005, p. 1578). Ageing hits the poorest countries hardest. Because more people die sooner of age-related disease in developing nations, these nations have the most to gain economically from having more healthy productive workforces. In fact, there are serious costs involved in poor public health which leads to increased instances of preventable deaths. One study researching the macroeconomics of death projected that the "value of lost output [arising from preventable deaths] resulted in a projected cumulative loss of $11.2 trillion in [low- and middle-income countries] during 2015–30, with a potential economic output loss of up to 2.6 percent of GDP in low-income countries by 2030," (Alkire et al., 2018). It appears that there is a strong humanitarian and economic case for solving ageing. Developing countries could realise greatest savings by enabling their people to live longer, happier, and healthier lives.

Another economic benefit to curing ageing would be that it obviates the need for expensive state-run old-age support systems. The primary justification for the existence of state-funded pension and elderly support schemes is that they are needed to protect aged persons from falling into poverty. States provide pensions on the presumption that individuals will not have the physical or intellectual fitness to continue serving in the labour force producing goods and services. In Canada, these elderly supports take the form of the tax-funded Old Age Security benefit and the Guaranteed Income Supplement as well as the Canada Pension Plan. These government programs are expensive. One study found that Canada Old Age Security expenditures are projected to peak at 2.39 percent of GDP in 2035, and total income support expenditures are projected to reach 3.12 percent of GDP in that same year (Globerman, 2021). Ending ageing would allow for the elimination of these expensive public support programs. For instance, old-age support funding savings could be reinvested into post-secondary subsidisation, the promotion of free enterprise, the reduction of taxation, and work retraining. Eliminating these programs would further allow for the reallocation of large amounts of existing money in large sovereign wealth funds. Norway's Government Pension Fund has US$1.3 trillion in assets (equivalent to almost 300,000 per Norwegian citizen) and continues to grow. There are similarly large funds in China, Saudi Arabia, and Singapore. Overall, curing ageing would open up money currently funding old-age supports that would offer excellent return on investment for taxpayers.

The preceding chapters focused on economic benefits of anti-ageing with respect to economic savings. We will now turn to look at how ending ageing could produce direct economic benefits. One probable economic benefit to ending ageing is that it would generate wealth and innovation. A cure for aging would unleash extraordinary innovation in several respects. For one thing, it would enable the greatest innovators to live indefinitely. Humanity often loses thinkers who would otherwise have created great works should they have been able to carry on their work with youthful vigor--think of Einstein whom we discussed earlier. A cure for ageing would not prevent new great minds from coming into being but it would preserve old ones. What is more, a cure for aging would drive people toward higher education, specialisation, and entrepreneurial risk-taking. There is a strong correlation between longevity and education. Studies have indicated that as one's educational attainment increases, their mortality risk declines (Hummer and Hernandez, 2013). The relationship between education and longevity could also be reversed. Individuals that have little expectation of living a long time are not rationally motivated to invest in lengthy and expensive educations. If individuals were confident they were going to live long, it is reasonable to expect that investment in training and education would become more attractive. In this way, ageing will be a driver of growth in education and re-training. Another interesting finding is that there is evidence that the sort of innovation that drives entrepreneurialism and free enterprise peaks in one's 40s (Weinberg and Galenson, 2005). The problem is that many older people feel lock-in to their career and family life and thus are unwilling to take risks compared to younger people. However, a cure for ageing could enable people to be more comfortable taking entrepreneurial risks given that they would have limitless time to regroup and try again and the opportunity cost of that time would be significantly lower on average. With more time, people would be more comfortable investing in longer education and in the creation of innovative products and services and this would produce economic growth.

However, a cure for aging is not only economic in that it would reduce deaths and promote health equality. It would free up medical resources and expertise that could be deployed to fight death and suffering unrelated to aging as well as help ensure individuals reach and sustain their peak levels of health. This would further compound the previously discussed economic benefits of living a long and healthy life. In 2019, the World Health Organisation profiled the leading causes of death around the globe. They found that 7 of the 10 leading causes of deaths (74% of deaths globally) were non communicable diseases that originated in ageing (WHO, 2020). A cure for ageing would lead to the disappearance of the vast majority of today's most deadly and frequently treated diseases, just like vaccines have virtually eradicated smallpox or polio. As a result of the end of ageing, nation's medical war chests could be productively redirected for spending in the fight against infectious disease, bodily trauma, rare and new disorders, neonatal diseases, and genetic abnormalities. While they are not the greatest causes of death today, these conditions are not trivial. People of all nations suffer under and die from these conditions in significant numbers. Millions of people, predominantly in poor countries, die from malaria, tuberculosis, HIV/AIDS, cholera, rotavirus, shigellosis, and typhoid every year. Ending ageing could mean freeing up resources to end other common types of death. Moreover, it could mean promoting healthy behaviour. Lifestyle choices could result in death, even given the invention of a cure for ageing. Health problems like smoking, obesity, heavy drinking, inactivity, and chronic poor sleep will endure, cure for ageing or not. However, resources could be re-deployed and invested in treatments and interventions to ensure maximum health. Indeed, individuals may be incentivised to maintain peak health if they knew it was essential to the indefinite extension of the life of their cells. It is clear, then, that an end to ageing could be a miracle for the health and wellness of mankind.

Another economic benefit concerning solving ageing is that it could have several radical impacts on consumer behaviour. For example, a cure for ageing has the potential to cause individuals to become more concerned about environmental health and ecological sustainability. If individuals knew they would live to feel the full impact of consumption-caused environmental degradation (such as overfishing, water pollution, or deforestation), their choices and consumption patterns may change. This may lead to innovation in commercial production and a reduction in costs associated with the bad ecological outcomes of climate change. Individuals change their behaviour when it imposes costs on them. For example, wealthy western countries have for most of the 2000's paid poor countries to act as dumps and receive mountains of plastic waste and trash for disposal. In recent years, many trash-receiving countries like China, Malaysia, and the Philippines have stopped or curbed the import of plastic wastes. This, in turn, has caused western countries to improve their recycling and waste management strategies as plastics could no longer be sent cheaply elsewhere to become someone else's problem. Similar changes in consumer behaviour could follow solving ageing. Another possible economic benefit of solving ageing could result from the accelerated decline of organised religion. Perhaps the main reason for the existence of organised religion is to make death less daunting. If involuntary death was the exception, not the rule, people may become less invested in religious fanaticism and tradition which subordinates their individuality. A cure for aging might lead individuals to explore their spirituality without clinging to a legacy religion for existential support. This would solve the economic problem which is that individuals who are heavily invested in religions can have their consumption and production suppressed as a result of their beliefs. There are too many examples of this to discuss presently. But, one may think of Muslims not consuming alcohol or recreational drugs, Hindus not consuming beef, and certain religions not embracing modern efficient technologies. The continued decline of religion could also have positive impacts in the growth of capital markets and free enterprise. Instead of paying religious dues, individuals may choose to invest significant portions of their income into stocks, bonds, currencies, financial instruments, new businesses, and other business ventures. This form of productively re-allocating resources could have compounding benefits for the economic welfare of people everywhere. Finally, while not related to consumer behaviour, the end of organized religion could lead to the abolition of tax breaks and incentives for religious organisations. Instead of allowing founders of religions and televangelists to jet-set and live glamorously without taxes, this otherwise missed tax revenue could be used for public benefit. Overall, ending ageing would be perhaps the most impactful event in human society and economy and these are merely a speculative sampling of the positive economic effects which could result.

Thus far, this chapter has only addressed the generally positive economic consequences of ending ageing. However, an event as impactful as solving ageing may have serious economic costs as well. The leading economic concerns around solving ageing are overpopulation and the potential for a resource depletion crisis. It is true that if everyone on Earth today suddenly adopted the consumption patterns of the average American, there would be a crisis of resource insufficiency. It is clear that wealthy nations use resources at rates dramatically higher than those in poor nations, where the vast majority of the population today lives. This concern appears to identify a valid economic problem. However, it may fail to recognise two key facts about markets and economics. First, population growth is slow and that populations will grow irrespective of a cure for aging. Second, Markets and consumption patterns adapt to changes in the supply and demand of resources. Let us first address the potential negative effects of population growth in a world where ageing is a medical non-problem. For one thing, it appears immoral to not deliver or develop life-saving therapeutics merely because they would increase the world population. It would be unreasonable to deny a cancer patient chemotherapy on the basis that their living would contribute to overpopulation. But, more practically, overpopulation is a myth and a non-problem. It may be true that too few individuals are living in a particular area that is not well-organised for their use. But it is false that population growth will continue unabated. Population growth is already slowing today. In the future, population growth will continue to slow and decline around the world even in fast-growing continents like Africa and Asia (United Nations, 2019). Indeed, the world population is set to peak in 2064 at 9.7 billion and then decline thereafter (Vollset, 2020). Individuals have fewer children when they are rich and educated.

Based on current trends of growth, it is clear that global dystopian overpopulation will not occur, cure for aging or otherwise. But what of the issue of resource insufficiency? For one thing, it is important to recognise that this issue is related to but not necessarily arising from solving ageing. The availability of resources will become an issue for discussion while populations get richer and demand more resources to achieve their desired quality of life. However, the size of this issue may be overblown. For every problem, there is a potential technology which offers a solution in order to produce more of a good efficiently or find a sufficient complement. The modern world, anti-aging or not, is not a world of shortage but a world of abundance. Our economic and social problems are in the distribution of goods, not their production. As David Sinclair points out, "We literally throw away half of the world's edible food each year, more than a billion tons of it, even as millions of people are left hungry or malnourished." (Sinclair, 2019, p. 32). And, even if a good could not be generated in abundance, markets and people would adapt to overcome the shortage. Resource depletion would not result from or be exacerbated by the invention of a cure for aging. Notwithstanding these arguments, it would be premature to conclude that a cure for ageing has no negative economic impacts as they may be hidden or only develop later.

The purpose of this chapter was to profile the potential economic effects of ending ageing as a disease. In particular, this chapter looked at the benefits and costs of healthcare, old-age supports, labour market engagement, economic efficiency, consumer behaviour, population growth, and resource consumption. In summary, this chapter had three broad themes. First, there will would be enormous savings in ending ageing because it would drive down costs in healthcare and old-age support. Second, a cure for ageing will have positive economic

effects in driving increases in entrepreneurship and education, reducing the negative impacts of age-unrelated health disorders, and driving beneficial change in consumer behavior. Third, ending ageing is a significant change in human life which could have negative economic impacts but will not cause or exacerbate problems related to overpopulation and resource depletion.
The cure for ageing will unleash positive benefits to people everywhere and is likely to most benefit the poorest in the world. On the whole, the economic effects of ending ageing need to be embraced and not feared.

Chapter 8
Ethical Issues With Eternal Youth

"Science and technology are the keys to both our longevity and our demise. Our entire existence on this planet is a double-edged sword."

-Rhys Darby

Introduction

As long a history and as many benefits as anti-aging pursuits and technologies have, it would be natural to assume that it is a field without many issues or concerns, at least relatively speaking. After all, when discussing fields dedicated to the extension of human life, it doesn't seem that there should be that many objections regarding their pursuits, or that there would be arguments against even the sci-fi, pseudo end goal of immortality. Despite any possible first impressions and the variety of benefits covered so far over the course of this book, though, there are actually a number concerns raised against the pursuit of anti-aging and immortality, including arguments concerning the ethics and obligations regarding the science and applications of it, concerns over equality and who would have access to breakthroughs in life extension, whether it is natural or right to want to further extend our lifespans and the damages that could actually come with doing so, as well as very practical yet grim concerns regarding what living significantly longer would mean for the world's population and resource consumption rates. All these concerns will be looked at here.

Population and Resource Concerns

While it may not be the most obvious or pressing concern when discussing extending the human lifespan by only a few years at most, concerns over the rate of resource consumption take on a greater level of significance when discussing more substantial increases to the human lifespan. As it stands, without even beginning to factor in any possible effects of an increased lifespan meaning people will be around longer to consume more, we are consuming renewable resources such as timber and wildlife at nearly twice the rate that can be sustained by the Earth. We are on track to be closer to three times the sustainable rate within just a few decades ("Resources and Consumption," n.d.). What this means is, based on trends starting back in the 1970s and how our rate of consumption has increased since then, we are already looking at using up renewable resources significantly faster than they can be replenished. Now, of course population growth is not the only factor contributing to this increased rate of consumption, and in fact it is believed that we do actually have enough resources to sustainably keep a population of 10 billion people going - something that would obviously require changes, and which would not be possible if we keep at the ever increasing rates of consumption we are currently at (Lucas & Horton, 2019). However, just based on what the Earth can actually provide us in resources, we could actually feed a population roughly 20% higher than what we have now. The thing is though, through natural population growth we would have some amount of time to make changes and improvements - not a lot of time mind you, since it's predicted the world population will be past 11 billion by 2100 (Lucas & Horton) - but time nonetheless.

Unfortunately though, it seems like the improvements we make don't always actually reduce our consumption rates; a study conducted at MIT examining how improving the efficiency of our consumption of over sixty materials found that, contrary to what might be expected, being more efficient in our consumption actually led to increased consumption rates of the vast majority of the materials (Chu, 2017). This finding was due to the fact that, thanks to lowered prices resulting from the improved efficiencies, consumption went up because of the increased demand for the now more affordable materials - a result found in the case of all but six of the over sixty materials examined ("Resources and Consumption"). So, as it is, we are on track to use resources at a rate multiple times past what the planet can sustain, our efforts to more efficiently produce and use resources quite often leads to more of the resources being used overall due to lowered prices, and we have less than a century to sort out these and other resource concerns before we reach 10 billion population, the rough limit of what we can sustainably feed if we make radical changes to how we deal with food. What happens if you make it so everyone lives an extra decade or two?

As can be seen by the issues just covered, we aren't necessarily in the best spot when it comes to resource usage or management as it is, and the predicted increases should nothing change don't look any better. So, odds are increasing how long everyone is around won't exactly have a positive impact on the above issues, or others so far left unaddressed, like those that would stem from people being around to not just consume for longer, but also to pollute. However, while population growth is a factor, it doesn't really seem to be the greatest, at least in regards to our consumption of food since we can apparently sustain almost 2.5 billion more people than are currently around with the proper changes. Given this, imagine we do actually make the changes needed to be sustainable. Imagine for a moment that we go so far as to become somehow even more sustainable than was suggested, allowing for a population of over 11 billion people to comfortably and sustainably live without resource concerns. Based on the present situation and numbers this doesn't seem that realistic of a scenario, but let's explore it for a moment anyways. At the time of writing this, almost 74 million people have been born this year, just over 31 million people have died, and we are expected to hit the 8 billion mark by 2023, with the 10 billion mark being projected for around 30 years from now in 2055 (Worldometer, n.d.). These numbers are obviously projections based on current trends and absolutely could change, but taken at these rates we have just over 30 years before we hit the population which we can feasibly and sustainably feed, and it's believed we will be past 11 billion by the turn of the next century (Lucas & Horton, 2019). If we were to add to natural population growth with further substantial life extensions, how will we manage? We are already set to be past capacity even in the unrealistic hypothetical proposed by the end of the century, meaning if all our numbers are even close to right we likely still wouldn't have even another 100 years before population becomes a concern, even if we fix just about everything else. How are we supposed to manage this?

One possible solution could be to limit how many children people can have through the implementation of a variant of the one or two-child policies that, while controversial, have already been put into practice in the past. In fact, it's possible that some version of this may even come to be naturally, as perhaps humanity will simply start having fewer children; in nature we often see that animals that live longer have fewer offspring (Traulsen & Mehnert, 2019), and with fewer time constraints thanks to living longer, maybe we will see this sort of shift somewhat naturally in the population, especially in the cases of particularly extreme life extensions ("Is immortality unethical?," n.d.). Unfortunately though, there isn't anything saying that this will necessarily be enough, or even the approach we end up taking. Currently more than twice as many people are born as who die (Worldometer, n.d.), meaning it could be quite difficult to somehow hit an equilibrium and keep the population stable around 11 billion in our idealized hypothetical, even if people do become less inclined to have as many children as often on their own due to increased lifespans, and that's without looking at how difficult it could be to achieve this sort of policy in the real world, whatever it may look like in 80 years time. Because of this, and who knows how many other possible reasons, people may end up taking more drastic approaches to population control in the future. While it certainly seems counter productive to increase the lifespan of people just to turn around and engage in some form of generational culling or 'cleansing' in order to manage population growth, it isn't exactly unrealistic to fear that at some point down the line, this may actually be taken as a solution. It seems possible that future people may find themselves trying to determine how long people should be allowed to live for in order to make room for future generations should we reach a point where the human lifespan has been significantly increased past what it is now, and we find ourselves running out of room (Than, 2006). However, as awful as some of this could be, it is all still just speculation. What isn't just speculation though is the state of our resources, the rates of their consumption, and the fact that they raise concerns for population growth as it is, let alone population growth due to the extension of the human lifespan. Unsurprisingly though, these aren't the only source of arguments which can be raised against keeping us around for longer.

Religion and Immortality

Our views on a topic can be influenced by any number of factors, and few factors can have as much of an impact on a person's outlook and views than their faith. As such, it probably shouldn't come as a surprise that views on anti-ageing are no exception. In fact, the impact of religious views and arguments isn't limited just to what they add to the discussion surrounding anti-ageing, as it has been found that religion informs people's views on aging in general (Ewen, Nikzad-Terhune, & Dassel, 2020). In the past, views on aging through religious lenses have shifted as the religions themselves did. Though American revivalists from the Victorian era viewed those who reached old age as being immoral - holding a belief that if they made it to old age it meant they hadn't yet been saved by Christ and were as such sinners - the Calvinists viewed the eldery who were still in good health and as such "useful" as being blessed by God (Ewen, Nikzad-Terhune, & Dassel). Unlike these two, Puritans in the United States had great respect for the elderly, and as our understanding of medicine, health, and longevity improved religious views of the eldery began to come more into line with the idea that living to old age meant one had been blessed and as such was a good thing (Ewen, Nikzad-Terhune, & Dassel). However, while old age is now more widely considered a blessing than an indication of wrongdoing, this doesn't necessarily mean many religions would embrace artificial life extensions with open arms. Beyond the fact that the particularly brief history of some religious views on aging only covered a handful of branches of Christianity, and as such are in no way indicative of or informative about the views of other religions, there is quite an immediate and apparent distinction between living to old age thanks to one's health, and being brought there through scientific interventions which without the person would have died years ago. As such, though still bringing people to old age, extending a person's life through science hardly denotes much of a blessing on that individual from above. Additionally, for many religions death is an important part of their faith, as if one has lived a good life they are rewarded at the end with a version of paradise or immortality, or in some cases another life. Many religions also discourage pursuits that only benefit the person themself, and in the case of Christianity, an argument can be made against anti-aging around the fact that, after being driven out of the Garden of Eden, humanity was cut off from the tree of life purposefully (Benzekri, 2020). As such, from this view it is reasonable to ask 'who are we to work against this deadline which has been imposed on us all?' Of course, that all being said, our lifespans are already longer today than they were in the past, so maybe future extensions to the human lifespan will end up being accepted the same way the ones we currently benefit from are.

Ethics of Anti-aging in Theory

Despite the many benefits that would come and have already come thanks to anti-aging research and practices, there are still a number of ethical concerns surrounding the topic within the scientific community. Two views which provide particularly significant criticisms towards the idea of extending the human lifespan are Equlitarianism and Natural Law; the former raises concerns regarding the pursuit of prolongevity due to the many inequalities and issues already present in the world and argues that this pursuit, if undertaken before the issues already at hand are dealt with, will add to many of them and ultimately increase class disparities (Post, 2004). The latter on the other hand raises concerns more so over the principle of the matter, as Natural Law criticisms revolve around assertions of the goodness of human nature and of aging, as well as arguments that extending the human lifespan will actually take away from the experience and significance of life (Post). Beyond these views though, there are still further arguments both for and against this pursuit, many of which are more focused on the science of it than the philosophy. Along with the previously mentioned concerns of overpopulation, and the just briefly mentioned concerns over how it will impact the state of the world as it is as well as our experience of life - as, if you're around long enough, eventually life itself may outlive its value (Mackey, 2003) - concerns have also been raised regarding the impact the practice could have on ageism (Mackey, 2003; Post, 2004), as well as the idea that we would be working against the natural course of things and potentially even substantially altering and commodifying ourselves (Mackey). Some of these have already arguably been addressed fairly well - the concerns of promoting ageism, for example, which have been argued against by pointing out that there isn't any reasonable connection between prejudice and anti-aging research, and if anything the research and practice would promote old age, since one of its aims is to make old life better for longer (Post). However, others are still somewhat greyer. One area of some fair deal of discussion is whether or not aging is a disease, or should be treated as one (Post, 2004; Woo et al., 2019). Without spending a great deal of time on the debate, the argument largely revolves around whether aging meets the criteria of being a disease or not, obviously, as well as whether this really means we should or shouldn't attempt to 'treat' it. One argument in favour of treating it one way or another is that working to combat ageing can help to slow down or maybe even prevent a number of age related diseases like cancers and alzheimer's (Woo et al., 2019), and as such there is good medical reason to treat it regardless of its own status as a disease.

Another interesting ethical argument is that, regardless of the potential impacts it may or may not have, there is an ethical obligation to pursue this line of research. Without looking too closely yet at the forms treatments may take, the argument has been made that there is a moral obligation to pursue anti-aging research and practices based on the principle of beneficence - the duty of physicians to work to help their patients and work for their benefit (Mackey, 2003; Post, 2004). Though it doesn't address most of the other ethical concerns regarding anti-aging research, this stance argues that it simply offers too much good to ignore or avoid, as while also extending a person's life, research aimed at slowing down aging shows promise with reducing the rate of many age related diseases, so much so that some argue that it outweighs the potential risks (Post, 2004). Along these lines, bioethicist John Harris puts the argument this way (Than, 2006):

> *It is one thing to ask, 'Should we make people immortal?' and answer in the negative. It is quite another to ask whether we should make people immune to heart disease, cancer, dementia, and many other diseases and decide that we should not.*

For Harris, the ability to combat these and other diseases brings too much good to ever turn down the pursuit of anti-aging research, even if extending the human lifespan carries with it promises of future issues. Of course, not everyone agrees with this stance. While some have additionally argued that the possibility that only subsets of the population will end up reaping the benefits of this research isn't reason enough to deny the benefits from them too, but others argue on the ground of distributive justice that this gives moral reason to not (Pijnenburg & Leget, 2007). Rather than viewing it as simply benefiting one small group of people and no one else in a sort of 'Haves' and 'Have-nots' fashion, this line of thinking argues that this doesn't simply benefit one without affecting the other, but actively brings about a more unjust and morally wrong situation, and says that by arguing about how to justify only some people getting access to it they lose sight of the larger moral issues (Pijnenburg & Leget). This will be looked at in some greater detail somewhat later in the chapter though, and for now the discussion will move away from arguments concerning the theory of the pursuit, and instead onto the ethical concerns of some possible ways the theory may be realized in practice.

Ethics of Anti-aging in Practice

Before briefly looking closer at some of the possible approaches and routes that could be taken to extend our lifespan and some of the concerns specific to them, we will first look at some of the more general concerns that could be relevant regardless of how the extension is achieved. No matter how we manage to allow ourselves longer lives here on the planet, whether through advances in decelerating aging, defeating it all together, or even more sci-fi outcomes like through the use of robotics, a lot of details and parts of life will remain relatively unchanged. As it is now, there are people at or nearing the end of their lives who don't care to be alive anymore who wish to end their lives and simply pass on. How to approach this issue still isn't universally agreed upon, as physicians are meant to do no harm, yet it can seem cruel to force someone to keep living in varying states of infirmity. If we were to achieve some sort of significant increase to our lifespan, then even if people end up with decades more of good, healthy life before the worst of aging sets in, many people will likely still find themselves in the same situation. In fact, because of the extra time they have, we may even see people reach this point sooner; anyone who was likely to be content with their life and ready for it to end early with a lifespan of just 90 or so years will likely feel the same if they were able to live for 140 years. Maybe they will find things to do until the same portion of their lives have been spent, but if they would have been content and ready to go after 90 years of life there is no saying that giving them 50 more will make them want to live them. After extensions, we may find ourselves with people who have had what used to be a long life, with several decades ahead of them left to go, but ready to die. This sort of problem would likely become worse the longer the lifespan is extended, as allowing us to live 150, 200, or 1000 years won't remove the fact that people will still die, people will still get hurt or maimed or crippled, people will get depressed (Than, 2006) - and after 100+ years of life, it wouldn't be surprising if a lot of people got bored or tired of life. Due these concerns as well as others, in order to move forward with a greatly increased lifespan we will likely have to come back and reassess or finally find some sort of answer to questions regarding how we view life, and in the case of the above concerns, the question of when, if ever, is it okay for someone to take agency over their life and end it. If we don't, we may find that letting us live longer will provide just as many years of hardship as it does joy, if not more.

Now that we've looked at concerns we will have to face regardless of the approach taken, let's look at some of the possible avenues, and some concerns inherent to them. When discussing treating aging, three goals of biogerontology can be identified, each presenting a different approach to the issue of aging and age related diseases: compressed morbidity, arrested aging, and decelerated aging (Gems, 2011). The goal of compressed morbidity would essentially be to find a way to treat and protect against age-related illnesses without actually intervening in the aging process. While quite nice, and avoiding the concerns associated with extending the lifespan greatly since it wouldn't, the odds of achieving this without looking at the aging process seem quite slim; though a variety of additional risk factors for many age-related diseases could be prevented or worked against, like inactivity and obesity, age-related diseases are understandably quite closely related to aging, and so far studies in labs have only been able to achieve the delay of some illnesses without extending the lifespan, not true compressed morbidity. Arrested aging is essentially stopping the aging process all together, and even reversing it in the extreme of the goal. However, as one could probably guess by such a lofty goal, this isn't anything more than just a slim possibility, and shouldn't be something to be expected anytime soon. Lastly, we have decelerated aging - slowing the aging process, delaying age-related illnesses, and allowing us to live longer as a result. Important to note with this goal though, is that it wouldn't remove age-related illnesses - though one would have more years to live and more healthy ones on top of that, decelerated aging would simply help push back the effects of aging, and odds are many people would die of age and ageing-related illnesses all the same, just later. Another important note is that this pursuit has no end; when you aim to cure a disease or permanently solve a health problem through some new treatment, the goal of your pursuit is clear - treat the issue and cure it. With decelerated aging, though, all one would ever achieve is delaying the inevitable, and pushing back when a person is likely to begin falling victim to the worst old age has to offer. Despite this fact though, the moral drive to help alleviate suffering due to these diseases would still be in part addressed and progress would be made - but the need to help would still remain, as people are still going to get the diseases. As such, there is arguably a never ending moral obligation to further decelerate aging in order to combat the suffering caused by these diseases, without any ability to ever actually solve them when you go down this path. This of course leaves the pursuit open to previously raised concerns with the pursuit of anti-aging and extending the human lifespan, and though the argument has been made that the moral obligation to potentially stave off suffering on such a wide scale outweighs any potential misgivings or concerns over increasing the lifespan, not everyone is convinced of this. Additionally, perhaps there are issues to be raised with the pursuit of a goal that will forever be out of reach, and with the idea of simply putting off problems as being sufficient - albeit never ending - treatment for them. Ultimately only time will tell.

Life, Justice, and Immortality

Concerns regarding how unlikely it is that people will have equal access to any groundbreaking life extension discoveries have already been touched upon throughout the other sections of this chapter. As such, though a significant source of ethical concerns - that finding a way to substantially increase the human lifespan will ultimately exacerbate many problems and injustices already present today - no more time will be spent on this topic. Related to this topic though are a number of other concerns which will be given some attention here. The first of these is less so a concern over the possible ramifications of the achievement of substantial anti-aging procedures or technologies and of their likely unequal distribution, and instead a concern regarding the approaches currently being made by those who stand to profit off of current research and any future developments. Though very likely not the norm for reputable groups doing real, solid research into aging and the variety of diseases that often come with it, there is still an unfortunate amount of inaccuracy, and even deception when it comes to some claims that are made about products; though certainly reasonable to be hopeful about one's work and to share when it seems to be working, it has become all too common for misleading claims and overly aggressive marketing to lead to false expectations regarding medications (Woo et al., 2019). Through striving to make as much profit as possible, an unfortunate amount of deceptive and misleading tactics have been employed, leading to claims that are oftentimes almost entirely unjustified, if not actually entirely unjustified. The second and last related concern that will be addressed is once more about the impact the development and release of significant life extension technologies. However, rather than focusing on the social impacts, this second topic is concerned with the impact such extensions would have on the nature and experience of life itself. One concern along these lines has particularly spiritual and religious roots, and focuses on the idea echoed across many different faith systems: a focus on self preservation and on oneself is no way to live a good, meaningful life (Pijnenburg & Leget, 2007). Even those who don't consider themselves particularly spiritual or part of any faith are likely familiar with this sentiment in one form or another - a good life is one where you are modest, one where you go out of your way to help others, one where you do things not just for yourself. As such, objections are raised against the pursuit of life extension on principle, as any focused on or obsessed with the prospect of living longer, if not forever, have likely missed or chosen to ignore these often echoed sentiments. Along these same lines is the concern that a longer life isn't necessarily worth living. "Living longer is valuable only if it results in living longer in meaningful relations" (Pijnenburg & Leget); due to our nature as social beings, without meaningful interactions and relationships with others it doesn't really matter how long you are around for. Rather than focusing on living longer, this argument suggests we should be focusing on how to live better, and on how to improve life and conditions as it draws to an end, not on how to put that end off.

Conclusion

The various fields that find themselves researching and working on combating aging and its associated diseases have done a tremendous amount of good; life expectancy has been steadily climbing over the years, and it seems like new and promising medicines and treatments are being discovered or progressed all the time. Though there are significant concerns and objections to any sort of blind pursuit of or push towards eternal youth or life, this fact shouldn't be lost or forgotten. The fact that there is as much debate and discussion surrounding the ethics of these developments and of the pursuit of the goal itself is a good sign, even if there aren't many solid or decisive conclusions. Because there is discussion regarding issues raised here as well as others, it means that to at least some extent what needs to be considered is. It's hard to say what the ultimate outcome of these discussions will be; do the possible benefits outweigh the potential risks? Can we morally choose to not pursue work that could add healthy years to people's lives, and potentially even help inform us of how to combat the diseases we would otherwise just be putting off, even if the risks are that doing so will exacerbate just about every social issue we face and further increase the disparity present in the world? Could the world even handle it if we did? Though it's possible that any one or two concerns mentioned here seem easy enough to address when taken on their own, when put together and looked at as a whole the issue becomes a lot less clear cut. Ultimately, we're left to wonder. We can work to improve things, we can contribute our knowledge and abilities to the discussion, we can go out of our way to further worthwhile causes that could potentially eliminate some concerns - in the end though, there is still going to be a lot left uncertain.

Chapter 9
A Blessing Or A Curse?

"Why do so many people yearn for an eternal life when they don't even know what to do with themselves in this brief one?"

-Sydney Harris

Introduction

Up until this point in the book, much of what has been covered has been about the positives of extending one's life. Though a number of ethical and moral objections and arguments against anti-ageing were discussed in the last chapter, where varying viewpoints and stances on how natural or right the pursuit of eternal youth is, we still have yet to explore why we desire to live forever in the first place, and whether or not this should actually be desirable. Thus, the main focus of this chapter will be the exploration of whether immortality truly is a blessing or simply a curse in disguise and - regardless of the outcome of the former exploration - why we are still so seemingly desperate to acquire it, despite all of the cautionary tales and objections found surrounding the subject. While not all inherently related or connected, all of the arguments discussed and points raised in this chapter will be to these ends; they will be compared, contrasted, and potentially even combined during this endeavour in order to examine the cases that have been previously made about the topic, and in an effort to potentially even come to something of a conclusion of our own. We will start by examining some of the cases made against the pursuit of immortality.

Now, as has already been discussed at somewhat great lengths in earlier chapters, humanity has been chasing eternal life for quite some time now. Despite this long history of seeking out immortality, though, humanity has seemingly spent almost as long telling stories meant to ward off the desire and pursuit of immortality. Though not a particularly old example, one many may be familiar with that briefly touches upon the subject comes from the 2006 film 300, in the form of a line said near the end of the film: "May you live forever" (Snyder, 2007). Taken out of context, one could quite reasonably assume this line had a happier, kinder connotation than it did in the film. However, rather than being a message of well wishes, Leonidas uses the statement as a curse upon the person who betrayed the spartans. To Leonidas and his fellow spartans the prospect of living forever means no opportunity to die gloriously and with honour in battle. The words uttered by Leonidas, ultimately, only serves as a curse and as a negative portrayal of immortality because of the beliefs of the spartans depicted in the film; there is no honour in living forever, and death is desirable over dishonour (Francese, 2018).

Another argument comes from a story more than a few millenia older than the 2006 film 300, the ancient greek story of Tithonus. In greek mythology, Tithonus was a Trojan prince who became the lover of Eos, the goddess of the dawn, after he was kidnapped by her (The Editors of Encyclopaedia Britannica, 2007). From here, Eos went to Zeus in order to request that he grant Tithonus eternal youth, so that he may live forever with her. However, while Zeus obliged this request, he did not grant Tithonus eternal youth to go alongside his immortality, damning him to age forever without ever being able to die (The Editors of Encyclopaedia Britannica). This take on immortality is seen repeated in two other works of note, one being Lord Tennyson's poem from 1860, named "Tithonus" after the figure just discussed, and the other being Jonathan Swift's 1726 book, Gulliver's Travels. The poem closely echoes the greek myth, except for it is told from the perspective of the immortal narrator who is suffering the same fate as the namesake of the poem. The narrator describes the horror, loneliness, and decay, both physical and mental, that he suffers from due to immortality (Sagar, 2018). Echoing Lord Tennyson's poem, though this time telling the story from the perspective of an observer, is Gulliver's Travels, specifically in the part where the titular character encounters the race of people known as the Struldbrugs. Initially the protagonist believes that the Struldbrugs are blessed, as he learns that they are a race born with immortality (Swift, 1726). However, it turns out that the Struldbrugs suffer from the same kind of immortality as poor Tithonus, as they never stop ageing, causing them to eventually suffer greatly as they become decrepit and insane. All three of these works provide the same interpretation of immortality, one where you are eventually cursed to suffer for the rest of existence, without any upside. In this portrayal of immortality, it is clear to see that it is in no way a blessing, as your natural life is extended without stopping or even delaying the process of aging, meaning you spend an eternity in increasing infirmity while only guaranteeing you won't die young - clearly a fate one wouldn't ever wish upon someone they cared for, and one that only the cruel would wish on anyone else.

However, as clear cut as this interpretation is when examined on its own, it raises some questions in the context of a discussion concerning human attempts to scientifically extend our lives. Foremost amongst these questions is this: how likely a fate would this be if we were to medically achieve immortality? Scaling the question down for a moment, this is equivalent to asking if our pursuits towards extending our lives will equate to simply extending our infirmity. In some ways, this can already be seen with current medicine; we have developed a number of ways to keep people alive past ailments and injuries in old age that would have guaranteed death a hundred years ago, yet in many of these same cases you aren't exactly guaranteed the best quality of life, simply an extension of it (Zitter, 2017). So, this raises a rather significant question: is immortality a worthwhile endeavour? These questions and concerns touch upon something referred to as the Tithonus Error - the belief that efforts to combat ageing and extend the human lifespan will simply result in an extension of the frailty experienced at the end of one's life (de Gray, 2008).

Although seemingly a quite reasonable fear - having any and all suffering that one may experience during the end of their days extended for the sake of being alive for a small while longer - this line of thought is referred to as an error for a reason. To begin with, what we described earlier isn't really related to anti-ageing or gerontology at all; the practice of extending one's life past events and ailments that would normally mean death, even for just a brief while, is not related to the field or practice dedicated to finding ways to extend human life on a wider scale, it's simply modern medicine being applied to save lives in the moment. So, though there are almost certainly situations where people are kept alive past the point where someone may rather just let their lives end, that is in no way due to anti-ageing. In fact, it is fairly apparent to those who study aging that extending one's life during infirmity isn't a particularly reliable way to guarantee someone a longer life, since you are still more susceptible to and at risk from a variety of dangers (de Gray, 2008). Though there has been some disagreement within the field about what exactly the main focus of study should be, with some having argued against what they saw as a focus on the study of lifespan instead of studying the process of deterioration that comes with aging and how to slow them (Pletcher, 2002; Williams, 1999), it is generally acknowledged that the most productive way forward would be to extend the duration of a person's healthy life (de Gray).

With this particular perspective in the field, along with the general lack of interest in extending the period of time where one is the least happy with life, there seems little reason to assume that any form of 'immortality' or drastic extension of the human lifespan would actually lead us to a Tithonus fate; rather it seems that what will most likely occur ,should we ever reach this stage of advancement, will be more akin to what Eos intended for Tithonus to be gifted with, an extended life not plagued with infirmity. As lofty and far-fetched as the idea of true immortality is, or even a drastic extension to the human lifespan, it is even more unlikely that we would ever find ourselves trapped in a situation like Tithonus's. As impossibly out of reach as the science to make us live forever seemingly is, the science to achieve this goal and then have us continue aging into frailty is even further.

A potentially more realistic argument against immortality and its pursuit comes from a more modern take of a gothic horror classic: the story of Dracula. As there have been many iterations of Dracula since his tale was first written by Bram Stoker near the end of the 19th century, the discussion here will focus on aspects highlighted in and arguments made about the 2020 TV series presentation of the character. In this version, the titular character is still an immortal vampire who has been around for quite some time before the events of the show, feeding on others in order to stay alive (Gatiss, Moffat, Vertue, & Irving, 2020). Where the show becomes relevant to our discussion is through its portrayal of the main character; Dracula is an immortal count with everything you stereotypically could ever ask for: wealth, power and, of course, a means to perpetuate his own existence for as long as he wishes. Despite having all this, Dracula is far from satisfied throughout the course of the series; though he has all the time in the world and is constantly pushing for more, his ambitions are never truly sated and he is always left wanting more, leading to a never ending lifetime without anything more than fleeting pleasures (Rogers, 2020). Needless to say, it is unlikely that this is a fate many would wish upon themselves or a version of immortality worth pursuing. Somewhat humorously, we find a similar argument against immortality at least partially presented in three rather dissimilar sources: an episode of the Twilight Zone, a passage from the Old Testament, and the philosophical arguments of a famous 20th century moral philosopher.

The episode of The Twilight Zone in question is "Time Enough at Last," and tells the story of one Henry Bemis who simply loves to read but never has the time in his everyday life to do so. However, this all changes for Mr. Bemis when he finds himself the sole survivor of a nuclear holocaust, meaning that he now has all the time he could ever want to do whatever he wishes. Finding that books from the library had also survived the catastrophe, Mr. Bemis settles down to begin reading like he so desperately had wanted to do when the unthinkable happens: his glasses break, leaving him alone in the world and unable to engage in the simple luxury of reading (Serling, Venable, & Brahm, 1959). Surprisingly similar in theme, the passage from the Old Testament referenced above is as follows:

> *God gives some people great wealth and honor and everything they could ever want, but then he doesn't give them the chance to enjoy these things. They die, and someone else, even a stranger, ends up enjoying their wealth! This is meaningless—a sickening tragedy. A man might have a hundred children and live to be very old. But if*

he finds no satisfaction in life and doesn't even get a decent burial, it would have been better for him to be born dead. His birth would have been meaningless, and he would have ended in darkness. He wouldn't even have had a name, and he would never have seen the sun or known of its existence. Yet he would have had more peace than in growing up to be an unhappy man. He might live a thousand years twice over but still not find contentment. And since he must die like everyone else—well, what's the use?

All people spend their lives scratching for food, but they never seem to have enough.

(New Living Translation Bible, 2015, Ecclesiastes 6:2–9).

Now, though these examples are not exact replicas of Dracula they still reflect the same argument against immortality; both highlight what plagues Dracula in his immortality, the inability to be satisfied in a life that is giving you everything you wanted. While these examples also demonstrate that this issue is not restricted to immortal life, the fact that it would be a source of misery for someone in a lifetime of only a hundred years further proves what an unpleasant fate it would be to endure for all of time. Whether over a single lifetime or over the course of as many lifetimes as will ever take place, being trapped in a life one is never able to enjoy or appreciate is far more a curse than blessing, and one where the only silver lining is that being trapped in such a life is simply a possibility, not a guarantee. When discussing eternity though, is that really a risk worth taking?

Bernard Williams, the aforementioned 20th century moral philosopher, based his arguments against immortality on a subject quite similar to the inability to be satisfied with or to enjoy life that is portrayed in the previous three examples - boredom

(Sagar, 2018). While it is simply a possibility that someone may find themselves never happy or sated in any life, immortal or otherwise, Williams argues that if a human life goes on long enough we would find ourselves suffering from unspeakable levels of boredom sooner or later, and even went so far as to compare an immortal life to being trapped in a cocktail party that never ends (Sagar). Williams makes this argument against immortality based on the concept of categorical desires, or desires that keep people going and give them a reason to live (Pereira, 2020). Categorical desires can be any number of things, including ambitions, dreams, or significant lifelong goals, just so long as they are a desire that keeps you wanting to be alive. However, in his argument, William claims that these desires are exhaustible; though if you were to live forever you would maybe be able to always find something to do since you are alive and there, you would eventually achieve or otherwise lose interest in every goal or dream that kept you motivated and going forward (Pereira). In this way, Williams argued that eventually an immortal's life would be devoid of any reason to continue going on (Pereira). To avoid being damned to an eternity of boredom, one might go out and acquire or find completely new interests and develop goals around them, but this solution raises new problems of its own as Williams doesn't just argue that categorical desires are critical to a life worth living, he argues that they are a key point of our identities (Rogers, 2020). Though additional discussions of the possibility of losing who you are after being around for long enough will be looked at in greater depth later, as it relates to Williams's arguments the exhaustion and subsequent replacement of all of one's categorical desires would entail a drastic change in who we are as individuals, and an abandonment of our identities equatable to the death of who we once were (Rogers). Following from this, how can one justify the pursuit of immortality for oneself if it will leave you either bored and miserable for all eternity, or will simply end up being for the benefit of what is essentially someone entirely distinct from who you are?

Though likely not all written or devised with the same purpose as Williams had when constructing his argument against immortality, we can find examples of what Williams argues in a variety of presentations of immortality. The first and least similar comes from the story of the famous ghost ship by the same name, The Flying Dutchman. Though there have been a variety of retellings and presentations of the story, whether they were cursed to never be able to make port or were only allowed to do so once every set number of years (The Editors of Encyclopaedia Britannica, 2017), a constant in the tale has been that the captain and crew were damned to sail the seas for all of time. Being the tale of a curse, it should be no surprise that this version of immortality is hardly a positive one, as all involved are damned to sail without rest, but what is interesting about the tale is that the curse of The Flying Dutchman is essentially a particularly specific example of what Williams describes immortal life to inevitably become: an eternity of repeating the same actions, here only sailing, without any meaning or joy.

This situation is likewise represented in Steven Spielberg's film, Indiana Jones and the Last Crusade (1989) in the form of the immortal knight guarding the holy grail. Though the knight himself is not necessarily presented as miserable in his eternity of isolation and singular duty, the situation he is in - that is, being alone in a room full of drinkware for all of time with nothing to do other than stand guard - is hardly one that many would presumably wish upon themselves or anyone they cared for. Though seemingly coping with immortality through sheer strength of faith and will, and as such presenting a minute possibility that maybe being bored for eternity isn't that bad, the

Knight's disposition has no great impact on the message of the scene and film, as the Knight himself even joins in to make it clear that the pursuit of immortality isn't worth the cost.

Last is an example included by Williams himself in his argument: the 1926 opera The Makropulos Affair, and specifically the story of Elina Makropulos (Sagar, 2018). Elina drinks an elixir which grants her immortality for as long as she keeps drinking it, and which keeps her physically at the age of 42 for the duration. However, after living for several centuries she finds herself having done and accomplished everything she ever wished to, leaving her without any further reason to live. As such, Elina decides to stop drinking the elixir and allow herself to die and escape the empty and boring existence she had found herself in. Having been used by Williams himself, the connection is immediate - Elina's situation is exactly that which Williams argues will eventually befall any immortal. While the other two examples simply highlighted the prospect of inescapable boredom, Elina's story highlights what happens when one exhausts all categorical desires and forgoes abandoning one's identity in order to find more.

Though well thought out, arguments have naturally been raised against as well as in support of Williams's arguments and view that any immortal life would eventually become unbearable. As most of Williams's argument rests upon categorical desires and his claims that they are both exhaustible and integral to our identities and remaining who we are, most counters to his arguments target these foundational claims. To begin, the claim that categorical desires are exhaustible, or at least the claim that all categorical desires are exhaustible, is not one that is universally accepted (Pereira, 2020). While Williams's claimed that all desires would either be exhausted or abandoned given enough time, others have countered with the suggestion of desires that seemingly would be inexhaustible, such as the desire to learn everything that you can and to pursue knowledge, the desire for personal growth and self improvement, and the desire to develop relationships. While arguments can likely be made for and against these as well as other potentially inexhaustible categorical desires, the counter to Williams's position still raises the question of whether the dismissal of all categorical desires as exhaustible may be slightly premature, and may have more to do with the individual immortal in question than categorical desires themselves. Along this same line of thought, others have proposed the idea that surely some categorical desires are recyclable, so that after enough time one may find purpose and meaning in life once more from a previously exhausted desire.

Questions have also been raised regarding whether boredom and developing new desires are really that awful. Regarding the former, odds are anyone could imagine examples of lives that are meaningful and worthwhile even if they bore the people living them to no end (Pereira, 2020). Imagine a gifted doctor who truly couldn't care less for the profession, but who chose to pursue it regardless due to the amount of good they could do with their talents - surely anyone would say that that life is a worthwhile one, even if it isn't necessarily satisfying to the person in question. Regarding the latter, arguments have been made saying that the drastic, identity altering changes that would be required of us in order to find new categorical desires aren't necessarily as significant as argued, and are actually not dissimilar from natural changes of interest and growth that already occur during the presumably worthwhile mortal lives we are all currently living. As a simple example, think about the difference in desires and goals you had as a young child compared to those you hold now - it is entirely possible that some have remained or the that the spirit behind them has stayed the same, but even if all are drastically different now than before it doesn't become reasonable to argue that your younger self had no good reasons to live since you are now pursuing things they potentially never would have imagined being interested in. So, though most counters to his reasoning aren't presented as conclusively as Williams's presented his arguments, most still serve to raise questions about whether an immortal life really necessitates the concerns that Bernard Williams claimed it did, and present the possibility that, at least regarding concerns of exhausting your reasons to live, perhaps an immortal life wouldn't be that bad.

Counters to Bernard Williams's arguments are of course not the only works to have been made in response to him, though, as Williams has received support directly and indirectly from following works on the topic. In direct support of his work, some have made arguments supporting a slight reinterpretation of Williams that aims to avoid many of the counters made against him. One such alteration to Williams's arguments is to suggest that his claims were not as absolute as they have often been presented as being, and that instead his arguments actually only support the notion that, while some people with certain characteristics and qualities might have no issue living an immortal life, there is no good reason to assume that you or the average person are one of these people who wouldn't suffer from the concerns Williams raised (Gorman, 2016). Additionally, some subsequent works attempt to focus on the spirit of the issues raised by the arguments for or against Williams's view, rather than on directly supporting or countering them. Some have argued that, even if Williams is incorrect in his claim that immortality would eventually lead us to become bored and detached from the world around us, it still is far from clear whether it is worthwhile to pursue or desire an immortal life simply on the basis that our mortality is a seemingly crucial part of how we connect to our lives and find meaning in them, and we have no real way of knowing what kind of affect abandoning this critical aspect would have on us - so is it worth risking the loss of the value it gives (Beglin, 2017)?

Bernard Williams of course did not and does not have a monopoly on the consideration and argumentation on the topic of immortality. One significant concern about immortality is whether it serves to give or remove meaning from our lives (Andrade, n.d.). The significance of our mortality and the role it plays in providing meaning to our lives makes the topic of immortality tricky - some argue that a belief in immortality or some form of lasting impact is needed to avoid losing all hope, and to help us survive in the face of the notion that if there's nothing afterwards then what is the point of anything (Andrade). Opposed to this, though, is the view that the finiteness of our lives is exactly what makes them meaningful, as we wouldn't appreciate our chances and experiences as much if we weren't painfully aware of the fact that we don't have forever (Heidegger, 1978). As such, this latter view counters that what we do would actually lose meaning and value if we were to live forever, and that nothing would matter to us quite as much anymore. This view can be seen across various forms of media, with Jorge Luis Borges's short story "The Immortal" being one example of particular note. In the story, the main character begins by seeking out the city of immortals and immortality of his own, only to find that the inhabitants had lost all motivation to do or achieve anything as they now had all of time to do it eventually (Borges, 1947).

Moral philosopher Samuel Scheffler takes this argument - that life gets its meaning from death - and expands upon it in his work, as he argues that life gets its meaning from death because everything we value only makes sense in the context of the limited, finite life that they arose from (Sagar, 2018). If we remove ourselves from this foundational context and somehow achieved immortality, Scheffler argues that we would lose something foundational to what makes us distinctly human; all our efforts would only serve to contradict and frustrate ourselves, as the achievement of immortality would grant us eternal life at the cost of truly being human. In this way, from Scheffler's stance were we ever to attain immortality, we would lose all of our reasons to want to extend our lives in the first place.

So far many of the arguments examined have had more to do with issues regarding what it would cost us to become immortal, and how we may or may not suffer simply due to the loss of our mortality, than the costs we would face if any one of us were to live the life of an immortal. Two works which highlight some of the most significant costs are the short story "The Mortal Immortal" by Mary Shelley, and Mikhail Lermontov's 1841 poem "Demon." The former explores the life of a man who becomes immortal after drinking an elixir, and as a result is forced to continue living as he watches everything he knows and loves die around him (Shelly, 1833). Though it may not be the first thing thought of when considering living an immortal life, it becomes quickly obvious that if you are the only one granted immortality, then you will have to go through your eternal life with the knowledge that you will always lose anyone who you ever begin to care about, and won't have anyone to go through eternity with. Lermontov's poem explores a similar topic: the idea that, in an immortal life, you would forever be alone and outcast, unable to ever get close to anyone (Lermontov, 1841).

Beyond the fact that there's no way of truly knowing how an immortal life would really work or fit into a modern day world where no one else is immortal, whether it was treated as simply an accepted fact of life or it was something that you needed to keep hidden for all of time, it is unlikely a single immortal individual would ever be able to find a place in a world where anyone you attempt to get close to is guaranteed to die and leave you alone once more, and where any attempts you make are hindered by this incredible difference. As awful as these fates would be, though, there is one important counter that needs to be noted: there's no guarantee that you would be the only one. If you were to somehow come across the opportunity to be the only immortal person, these are things that you would be guaranteed to face, but any method of functional or actual immortality that we would ever develop would likely not be limited to one single person. It may be limited to only a small group of people, like those who found it or any who could afford it, but odds are eventually anything produced towards this end would be available to you and your loved ones.

This counterpoint, if immortality were to be achieved it would likely affect more than one single person, is actually quite significant when considering many of the possible downsides to immortality. If you're with your loved ones and existing indefinitely, maybe you lose yourself or change along the way, but you won't ever lose them, or at least if you do you'll have all the time in the world to get them back. Many of these downsides are at least lessened by framing the discussion around humanity becoming immortal, rather than any one person becoming immortal. Of course, this doesn't solve every problem - we would still have to confront concerns over the exhaustion of our categorical desires, issues of losing our reason to live, and maybe even something critical to being human, and just about everything else discussed by and in the wake of Williams and Scheffler. None of these concerns are solved by changing it to an immortal world instead of an immortal person. Likewise, whether it is just you or everyone who becomes immortal, concerns of damning yourself to an eternity of suffering would arise as any unpleasant or awful situation one may find themselves in could potentially be extended forever. Additionally, if you are around for all of time, then you are guaranteed to see every awful thing that may happen in the future. As such, while it appears quite likely from earlier discussions that being the only immortal would be an awful fate, granting immortality to all of humankind might not be that much blessing either.

With all of these concerns and downsides of immortality, they beg the question of why we have been searching for immortality, whether it be only for ourselves and maybe a small group of others, or for all of humankind. In light of all the risks and pitfalls, what drives such a desire? A want for power and time enough to get it? The desire to experience all that life has to offer even though, by all accounts, it seems you'll hate or at least be bored of it before too long? Or maybe it is some sort of likely misguided belief that, if we were to achieve immortality we would not find ourselves suffering from these possibilities, and that we would find a way that no one has thought of to keep meaning and value and joy alive with us for all of time. Maybe most people don't spend this much time thinking about it and so don't think of the downsides. All are possible and are likely to have motivated individuals in their pursuit or desire for immortality, but none seem likely to be the explanation of why humans have spent so long fascinated with it.

Odds are a significant portion of this desire comes from a fear of death - a fear of the unknown and leaving this world early - in spite of all the various arguments against fearing death. But there's something more than just the fear of death present in this desire, something which is captured by Basque philosopher Miguel de Unamuno in his book Tragic Sense of Life (1954) - and that is anger. When discussing his desire to live and to keep living forever, Miguel de Unamuno is outraged at the idea of dying, at the idea of wanting to die, and at the thought of having the center of his universe and the center of the universe to him, his "I" stolen from him (de Unamuno, 1954). In his passion, we see that it is not simply fear of death that motivates his desire to live, nor simply anger at the fact that he was doomed to die the same way that we all are, but anger at having his life stolen away (Sagar, 2018). As such, it becomes clear, and perhaps even relatable, that what upset him and fueled his passion so was this attack on his agency, this idea of dying before he was ready and being utterly helpless to do anything to stop it. This kind of passion and sentiment can actually be seen throughout various tales in Western culture, where, when confronted by the Grim Reaper, you are given an impossible chance or challenge or game, and if you best Death in whatever contest is presented to you, he has to let you go (Sagar). In this way, death is no longer something entirely out of your hands, as stories like these give back control and agency of one's fate; however slim their chances may be, they still have a chance to come face to face with death, and win.

Perhaps a desire to live forever isn't just understandable, but reasonable too. Chances are, no one wants to be stuck alive forever, for while that removes one thief of agency, it introduces another: with true immortality, you trade any risk of dying before you are ready for an inability to die at all, regardless of whether you are ready or even want to centuries or millennia down the line. As mentioned nearer the start of this chapter though, should we ever achieve a sort of functional immortality, or more likely simply further extensions to the human lifespan, odds are we wouldn't be trapped in it.

This kind of idealized immortality, or 'death upon desire' can actually be seen in the ancient Sanskrit epic Mahabharata, where the great warrior Bhishma is granted it (Sagar, 2018). Then, upon being impaled and stuck upon a bed of arrows after falling in battle, he decides he is not quite ready to die, and waits until he has passed on his knowledge to another before allowing himself to pass on. Should Bhishma have been granted immortality and if unable to be removed from the arrows or to recover from them, his boon surely would have become a curse, living in agony for the rest of time. Instead though, Bhishma had the opportunity to make peace with his end and ready himself before then, and only then, allowing himself to die. While of course both this and immortality are unlikely to ever be anything more than fantasies, created and held onto for the sake of easing our fears of what awaits us at the end, the distinction between them remains important. While immortality seems to be a curse at worst and a mixed bag that will vary depending on who is experiencing it at best, Bhishma's boon is simply a boon. Of these two it is easy to see that, though both are well confined to the realms of imagination, it is the latter that bears the greatest resemblance to anything we may achieve through the science of anti-ageing.

To sum up, it's difficult to truly and with certainty determine the nature of immortality. From the exploration presented here, it seems that there are quite a few more negatives than positives, but with a potentially infinite number of possible forms for immortality to take, ranging from the cursed existence of poor Tithonus all the way to some sort of possible utopia on earth, only the broadest of arguments for and against immortality are able to stand consistently, and they likewise all have their flaws. However, though uncertainty remains regarding the nature of immortality, hopefully it is fairly clear that it is far from equatable to any human endeavors at extending our natural lifespan. As such, though certainly interesting and providing plenty of food for thought regarding human nature and experience, the flaws and arguable nature of immortality as a curse are not inherently shared by anti-ageing practices.

Chapter 10
Alternative Routes To Immortality

"If you ask what is the single most important key to longevity, I would have to say it is avoiding worry, stress and tension. And if you didn't ask me, I'd still have to say it."

-George Burns

Over the course of the past two chapters, a variety of arguments against immortality - some on the grounds of ethical concerns, others against the desirability of immortality itself - have been presented and, to some extent, countered. Despite this previous exploration though, what exactly any form of achievable immortality would look like has yet to be fully addressed. After all, it becomes rather difficult to truly assess immortality as a blessing or a curse when all we can conclude about it is that immortality will entail living forever. Ultimately we are left with the uncertain nature of what form immortality would take in our modern day world. With the aim of clearing up what exactly immortality could look like for us, this chapter will focus on exploring various routes and alternatives to conventional immortality (simply existing while undying and unaging, like the Gods of ancient Greece) that we may one day actually reach as a species.

The 'Default'

The first and most obvious possible route to a kind of functional immortality is through the extension and arguable perfection of the broader topic of this book: anti-ageing. However, given that it has also been the focus of the majority of the rest of chapters, and that the focus here is on alternative routes to immortality and not simply the 'default,' the immortality that could come from work with anti-ageing and the ageing process itself will only receive a small amount of attention here. While of course a far ways off (if ever), the progression of the sciences of anti-ageing and longevity could possibly find the way to simply 'turn off' ageing, and halt senescence altogether. Despite this research, this concept is presently more science fiction than science (at least for humans). Though still largely a mystery across the board, scientists have identified a number of animal species that exhibit something called negligible senescence, or simply put, animals that don't show any evidence of biological ageing. One such animal is the cancer resistant naked mole-rat which generally lives up to 20 years, five times longer than other rodents their size, and where the oldest recorded was 37 and was still alive as of January 2020 (Lee, Smith, Buffenstein, & Harries, 2020). Now, as is easily noticed by the fact that they still normally only live for around 20 years, naked mole-rats and other negligibly senescent animals still aren't really immortal; though as far as we can tell these animals don't show any signs of biological degradation or slowing down with age, we still don't fully understand how or why the processes work out the way they do. Besides our immense curiosity, but ultimately limited understanding about the aging process or lack thereof, the animals can still die from any number of other means besides ageing, as many still get diseases, or are preyed upon, or sometimes even starve to death, especially in the cases of some which seemingly continue to grow indefinitely. All of that being said though, it is still an incredibly promising line of research, and one that gives hope that at some far off point in the future after we've uncovered the mysteries of aging and negligible senescence, we'll be able to 'turn off' the aging process, and potentially make humans negligibly senescent and functionally immortal.

The Soul and Life After Death

Though not necessarily the first thing people think of when discussing different forms of immortality, one of the oldest and lasting ideas of immortality comes in the form of beliefs about what happens to us after we are dead and gone. Rather than considering an immortal life in your physical body, at least as far back as Homer in ancient Greece people were discussing the idea of the soul, and how it lasts indefinitely past the expiration of our physical bodies (Lorenz, 2009). More broadly speaking though, the soul in both philosophy and religion is defined as "the immaterial aspect or essence of a human being, that which confers individuality and humanity … [and] which partakes of divinity," in the case of theology (The Editors of Encyclopaedia Britannica, 2020). In this way the soul is essentially the immaterial core of a person, one which persists after we're gone, and which potentially has been around as a concept in one form or another even amongst prehistoric peoples (The Editors of Encyclopaedia Britannica). Given the nature of the soul and the extreme longevity of the concept, it should come as no surprise that it represents a model of immortality all of its own. With as many cultures and faiths as there are which have some kind of notion regarding the soul, there are quite a few variations regarding what happens to the soul after it departs the deceased - some common examples likely familiar to most would be things like the various underworlds of ancient Greek and Egyptian mythologies which make up the afterlife in the cultures, or beliefs from Christianity which holds that the immortal soul goes on to be judged and spend eternity in either Heaven or Hell. Regardless of the exact belief, the broader model of immortality based around the human soul is this: people are made up of two distinct substances, the body and some kind of immaterial soul, the latter of which persists indefinitely in some form of space after the death of the former (Andrade, n.d.). Thanks to the philosophical contributions of Descartes and dualism in the 17th century, the soul is now often considered as one and the same with the mind as being the immortal aspect of a human being which exists regardless of any destruction of our physical bodies (Andrade, n.d.; Hasker & Taliaferro, 2019). As already mentioned, though the idea of the soul lasting indefinitely is shared across many cultures and faiths, the exact interpretation of the soul varies to some extent. Both ancient Egyptians and ancient Chinese people believed in the idea of a soul made up of two parts; for the ancient Egyptians, the ka lasted after death but remained with the body while the ba went on to the afterlife, and in much the same way for the ancient Chinese the lower soul would be lost upon death, while the hun would persist and be what was worshipped in the practice of ancestor worship (The Editors of Encyclopaedia Britannica). Hinduism and Buddhism, as well as some ancient philosophers separate from these faiths, believe that the soul not only persists after death, but that instead of existing in some space or afterlife or another indefinitely the soul persists for only some time before returning to a new body (Andrade, n.d.) - this of course is belief in reincarnation, a topic which will be returned to and explored in greater detail a little later. Then, just as a brief mention, the ancient Greek people had a variety of beliefs and variants of the soul thanks to the works of a number notable writers and philosophers, including the early Homeric version previously mentioned, as well as different ideas of the soul coming from Plato and Aristotle, just to name a few (Lorenz, 2009).

Quite intimately related to the idea of the immortal human soul is the idea of an afterlife in general. Though in many cases, like all those mentioned in the previous discussion, the human soul is what goes on to experience the afterlife, this is not necessarily true for all of them. While certainly conceptually similar, there is another model of immortality relating to the existence of two bodies that humans are made up of, rather than one body and one soul. In this model, there is the physical body capable of experiencing and acting upon the world and there is one called the astral body, made of some sort of other kind of substance (Andrade, n.d.). Despite having its place in a variety of what is considered more primitive religious thought, this model of an astral body which, much like the various forms of the soul, separates from the physical upon death and remains long after the physical body has passed hasn't really ever struck a chord with philosophers or theologians - though it is the basis of the idea of ghosts (Andrade). Unlike the concept of the soul, the idea of an astral body or self which detaches but remains ends up being more complicated, raising issues and leaving itself to be more easily dismissed. Two more significant issues that lead to this model's dismissal are: if the astral body detaches from the physical body at death, why can it not be seen doing so at the time of death? Secondly, and arguably more damning, the idea of the astral body or ghosts remaining and being seen tends to involve them appearing clothed, raising the notion that it's not simply an astral body that has remained, but some form of astral clothes too which cause the perceived astral bodies to be wearing them (Andrade) - an idea which feels too absurd to really write any great length about. This all being said though, this model of immortality via and astral body flaws and all is still just that - a model, and there is nothing necessitating that this model is all encompassing regarding these or other parapsychological topics. The fact that the astral body model is generally viewed as flawed and dismissed because of these flaws doesn't change the fact that people continue to experience or claim to experience things like the astral body; over time, many have tried to collect and verify accounts of mediums and the appearance of ghosts, and though a great number have been reliably and often even easily debunked, the fact that so many have and continue to occur raises the question of whether one truly can just outright dismiss the accounts (Hasker & Taliaferro, 2019). Regardless though, whether holding a grain of truth or completely void of anything resembling reality, the notion of a spirit or astral body lingering after the passing of the physical is one that has been with us for quite a long while, and constitutes yet another group of possible, yet somewhat more abstract realizations of immortality.

As mentioned briefly before, one last alternate and unconventional route to immortality is through reincarnation: the "rebirth of the aspect of an individual that persists after bodily death—whether it be consciousness, mind, the soul, or some other entity—in one or more successive existences" (The Editors of Encyclopaedia Britannica, 2021). Though there have certainly been a variety of takes and portrayals of it, odds are this definition of reincarnation - as being the concept of people persisting past death in order to be reborn in some form or another - is familiar enough to most. Though also included under the scope of parapsychology in the case of moments where people, generally under hypnosis, 'recall' events from a life they believe to be other than their own current one, as well as in the cases of children who have 'recalled' events or details about deceased people they shouldn't reasonably be able to know (Andrade, n.d.), reincarnation has also been part of many religions as an explanation for what happens after death. For starters, a number of Eastern religions have reincarnation as a part of their belief systems, with the role it plays and the form it takes varying depending on the faith. Both Hinduism and Jainism believe in reincarnation as a cycle, with one's past karma dictating how they are reborn, however the faiths take two different approaches to this cycle: for the former, everyone is born and reborn because of the desire for the limited happiness that can be gained through worldly pleasures, and while not all are viewed as sinful or wrong, these worldly pleasures will ultimately never give a true sense of enjoyment ("Reincarnation," 2019). As such, eventually this will lead one to pursue higher forms of happiness through spiritual experience and understanding, ultimately leading to the abandonment of the desires causing them to stay in the cycle of birth and rebirth, and leading them to a sort of salvation. Jainism on the other hand, though still teaching the importance of karma in determining one's reincarnation, also teaches asceticism so that one may eventually be free of all past karma, and frames it as the attempt to escape the cycle of birth and rebirth and achieve perfection by removing oneself from worldly and karmic concerns ("Reincarnation"). In Sikhism, reincarnation is not so much a process of one's soul eventually growing tired of what the world has to offer and then seeking enlightenment, but instead one that the soul must undertake in order to achieve a union with God; if one fails to perform righteous deeds in their life though, their soul won't be able to carry on to the next step in this evolution of the soul, and should they continue in this way they will become stuck in the cycle ("Reincarnation"). Of the Eastern faiths that will be discussed here, Buddhism's portrayal of reincarnation is the most different - rather than a cycle where the self seeks out worldly pleasures until it grows tired of them, Buddhism presents reincarnation as a method to perpetuate the suffering that is everything from birth to death. In Buddhism, there is no immortal lasting self that is reborn into a new body, but that instead it is more like a continuation of existence even after death, and even without the personality which made the person ("Reincarnation"). As such, the goal of Buddhism is to achieve Nirvana through overcoming and freeing oneself from their worldly desires so that they may escape this cycle. Despite the differences amongst these and other religions' views on reincarnation not discussed here, the belief that the immortal part of humans - and in some cases all things - go through a cycle of life and death, before eventually achieving eternity in paradise is yet another example of how some people have and still do pursue immortality

Immortality Through Technology

Moving away from the somewhat more abstract and faith based routes to immortality, we will begin this section with something somewhat similar to reincarnation that is offered via technology: cryogenic freezing, with the hope of one day being brought back. Though the field of cryogenic freezing encompasses more than simply freezing people with the intent of restoring them at a later time (see chapter 1 for a discussion of the other applications of cryogenic freezing), it is this use which will be focused on here, as it provides a sort of pseudo immortality. Cryonics is the practice of freezing and storing bodies, and technically corpses by current definitions, with the hope of one day being able to revive them (Andrade, n.d.). Assuming the technology is developed to restore cryogenically preserved bodies in the future, cryogenic freezing will allow us to indefinitely extend a person's life by preserving them, allowing them to be around and see things well past when they normally would have died. To some extent, this makes the process of cryogenic freezing somewhat akin to a technological cycle of reincarnation - should the technology be developed to revive cryogenically frozen individuals, people will be able to be restored and frozen, instead of being reborn and dying, potentially as many times as they should wish it. In this way, people can engage in a sort of cycle of restoration instead of reincarnation, allowing them to stay as long as they like before going under again to wait for another later time, even allowing individuals to stay in the cycle until they grow tired of the future worldly desires. This of course, as already said, is not any true form of immortality though. A key distinction between reincarnation and this proposed cycle of restoration is that the latter has a timer on it; though one's soul can be reincarnated for as long as one wishes to continue facing the world and all it has to offer, whether that be limited joys or suffering depending on your view of reincarnation, inevitably someone who is cryogenically frozen must die. Even if you drag it out over several thousand years, sooner or later your body will expire during one of your restored instances, and this artificial cycle will be brought to an end. Despite this though, cryogenic freezing may still be our best bet at lasting to see a thousand years from now, even if we would have to spend most of it frozen and dead by present definitions in order to get there. That being said though, it isn't the only route made possible to us through present and possible future advancements.

Another potential avenue to immortality comes from the particularly sci-fi idea of using technology to preserve our consciousness and selves past the point of our bodies' expiration. In theory there are a number of different ways technology like this could be developed, with one recent portrayal of note coming from the 2018 tv series Altered Carbon. The premise of the show is that the technology to store one's mind on a chip like device called a stack has been developed, meaning that so long as one's stack remains undamaged a person can survive past the death of their body, potentially to be put into a new body to live once more. Although again a very sci-fi idea - everyone having 'stacks' in them that can be swapped from body to body and which keep you alive past death - it is actually one that has received some amount of real world attention. For some scientists, the idea that one day we may be able to 'upload' our minds or otherwise emulate them with artificial intelligence has been considered an actual possibility, not just fiction (Kurzweil, 1993; Moravec, 2003). Of course, this isn't a view that is universally held; some question the idea that we would ever truly be able to make an AI capable of consciousness, as well as the idea that, even if we could make a conscious program, would we ever actually be able to carry over everything that makes someone who they are (Andrade, n.d.). Regarding the first question, about whether we could ever really make a conscious and understanding program, one significant counter comes from the 'Chinese Room' argument, a thought experiment which, in short, argues that a computer won't ever be able to understand anything because no input will ever actually have meaning to it (Hauser, n.d.). For those interested the entirety of the experiment - and how it compares a computer to a person doing a task involving a language they do not speak, using various script analogues which instruct and enable the person to complete the task effectively without understanding a word of it - it is certainly worth looking into it and the back and forth discussion surrounding it, as no great amount of time can be spent on the details and discourse surrounding it here. For our purposes, all that needs to be known is that, though some feel strongly that one day we will be able to make real conscious AIs, others question if it is even possible to achieve more than extremely complex and convincing simulations of consciousness, let alone ones capable of capturing the entirety of an individual.

The last avenue to life extension and possible immortality that will be explored here is actually quite similar to what was just discussed. However, rather than replacing our failing organs and body parts with machines, what if we could simply always easily replace them with healthy, working versions of themselves? An idea like this is explored in Nancy Farmer's novel The House of the Scorpion, where a drug lord called El Patrón has his failing health combated by constantly replacing them with younger healthy ones any time he has a health concern. However, the drug lord isn't the main character of the book; instead of focusing on the powerful criminal, the story actually revolves around someone meant to be a source of fresh, healthy organs should they ever be needed: El Patrón's clone (Farmer, 2002). Now, obviously everyone having clones of themselves for the sole purpose of slaughtering them and taking their organs is not a particularly pleasant future, and definitely far from an ethical one, but it may be possible that a similar end result could be achieved without the need of essentially farming humans. Though presently a somewhat controversial idea, the use of human embryonic stem cells have been proposed as a possible way to essentially clone human organs without needing to clone and harvest a younger version of yourself (Sandeep, 2018). However, as mentioned this idea is somewhat controversial, as the removal of the stem cells from the embryo ends up destroying the embryo, leading to discussion abouts the ethics of it (Conger, 2008). This all being said though, cloning human organs is ultimately a particularly complicated endeavour that research and work is still being done on. It's possible that in the future some development could be made allowing for the controversy to be avoided entirely by enabling the extraction of the stem cells without destroying the embryo - some ideas for which have already been proposed (Cascalho & Platt, 2006). Regardless, should a method for cloning human organs be fully developed and implemented, it could potentially open the doors to any number of additional ways to extend human life, perhaps eventually even to the point of immortality.

Conclusion

While not necessarily a comprehensive list of every possible route to immortality, whether they be based in faith, science, or some great deal of fiction, this chapter covers some of the more noteworthy and possible paths. Despite the promise and attention many of these receive though, it's difficult to determine if any will truly come to fruition. In the case of religious or spiritual paths to achieving immortality, the faith that you have in them is likely the closest thing to confirmation of your beliefs that you will get, at least until it comes your time to find out what, if anything, waits on the other side. And in the case of scientific routes to immortality, many are still more questions and theories than answers and proof, and it's entirely possible that the most that will come from them is new ways to extend life - not ways to prevent it from ever ending. Just as was the case with whether immortality is worth achieving or not, it seems there's no great certainty regarding whether or not we'll ever even have the chance to achieve it in the first place. Unlike whether it would be a blessing or not though, there seem to be a great many more possibilities that, at the very least something in the direction of living forever could come from some of these paths, even if none ever reach the real thing.

References

Alkire, B. C., Peters, A. W., Shrime, M. G., & Meara, J. G. (2018). The Economic Consequences Of Mortality Amenable To High-Quality Health Care In Low- And Middle-Income Countries. *Health affairs (Project Hope), 37*(6), 988–996. https://doi.org/10.1377/hlthaff.2017.1233

Anderson, R. M., Shanmuganayagam, D., & Weindruch, R. (2009). Caloric restriction and aging: studies in mice and monkeys. *Toxicologic pathology, 37*(1), 47–51. https://doi.org/10.1177/0192623308329476

Andrade, G. (n.d.). *Immortality.* Internet Encyclopedia of Philosophy. https://iep.utm.edu/immortal/

Andreas K, Stefan S, Jean-P W, Josef Z. (2020). Fatal attraction? Extended unemployment benefits, labor force exits, and mortality. Journal of Public Economics, Volume 191, 2019.

Andrews, M. D. (2004). Cryosurgery for Common Skin Conditions. American Family Physician University School of Medicine, 15;69(10):2365-2372.

Ai, A. L. (2006). Daoist spirituality and philosophy: Implications for holistic health, aging, and longevity. Holistic approaches to health aging: Complementary and alternative medicine for older adults. New York, NY: Springer, 149-160

Arrison, S. (2013). *100 Plus: How the Coming Age of Longevity Will Change Everything, from Careers and Relationships to Family and Faith.* New York: Basic Books.

Barzilai N, Atzmon G, Schechter C, et al. (2002). Unique Lipoprotein Phenotype and Genotype Associated With Exceptional Longevity. JAMA. 2030 doi:10.1001 jama.290.15.2030

Beyret, E., Liao, H. K., Yamamoto, M., Hernandez-Benitez, R., Fu, Y., Erikson, G., Reddy, P., & Izpisua Belmonte, J. C. (2019). Single-dose CRISPR-Cas9 therapy extends lifespan of mice with Hutchinson-Gilford progeria syndrome. *Nature medicine, 25*(3), 419–422. https://doi.org/10.1038/s41591-019-0343-4

Biography.com (2020). Elizabeth Bathory Biography. The Biography.com website. A&E Television Networks. https://www.biography.com/crime-figure/elizabeth-bathory.

Beglin, D. (2017). Should I choose to never die? Williams, boredom, and the significance of mortality. *Philosophical Studies, 174,* 2009-2028. https://doi.org/10.1007/s11098-016-0785-1

Benzerki, C. (2020, May 6). *Ethical reflections on immortality.* Think For Impact. https://thinkforimpact.com/2020/05/ethical-reflections-on-immortality/

Blagosklonny M. V. (2017). From rapalogs to anti-aging formula. *Oncotarget, 8(*22), 35492–35507. https://doi.org/10.18632/oncotarget.18033

Bloom, D.E., Chen, S., Kuhn, M., McGovern, M.E., Oxley, L., Prettner, K., 2020. The economic burden of chronic diseases: Estimates and projections for China, Japan, and South Korea. J. Econ. Age. 17 (2020), 10016. https://doi.org/10.1016/j.Jeoa.2018.09.002.

Bonkowski, M. S., & Sinclair, D. A. (2016). Slowing ageing by design: the rise of NAD+and sirtuin-activating compounds. *Nature reviews. Molecular cell biology, 17*(11), 679–690. https://doi.org/10.1038/nrm.2016.93

Borges, J. L. (1947). *The Immortal.*

Britannica, T. Editors of Encyclopaedia (2020). Ashkenazi. Encyclopedia Britannica. https://www.britannica.com/topic/Ashkenazi

Callaway E. (2020). 'It will change everything': DeepMind's AI makes gigantic leap in solving protein structures. *Nature, 588(*7837), 203–204. https://doi.org/10.1038/d41586-020-03348-4

Canadian Institute for Health Information. (2021). *Health spending.* Retrieved from CIHI.ca: https://www.cihi.ca/en/health-spending

Cardona, B. (2008). Healthy Ageing Policies and Anti-ageing Ideologies and Practices: The Exercise of Responsibility', Medicine, Health Care and Philosophy 11(4):475–83.

Cascalho, M., & Platt, J. L. (2006). The Future of Organ Replacement: Needs, Potential Applications, and Obstacles to Application. *Transplantation Proceedings, 38*(2), 362-364. https://doi.org/10.1016/j.transproceed.2005.12.055

Centers for Medicare & Medicaid Services. (2021). *National Health Expenditure Data.* Retrieved from CMS.gov: https://www.cms.gov/Research-Statistics-Data-and-Systems/Statistics-Trends-and-Reports/NationalHealthExpendData/NationalHealthAccountsHistorical#:~:text=U.S.%20health%20care%20spending%20grew,For%20additional%20information%2C%20see%20below.

Chaix, A., Zarrinpar, A., Miu, P., & Panda, S. (2014). Time-restricted feeding is a preventative and therapeutic intervention against diverse nutritional challenges. *Cell metabolism, 20*(6), 991–1005. https://doi.org/10.1016/j.cmet.2014.11.001

Chen, L., Hong, W., Ren, W., Xu, T., Qian, Z., & He, Z. (2021). Recent progress in targeted delivery vectors based on biomimetic nanoparticles. *Signal transduction and targeted therapy, 6*(1), 225. https://doi.org/10.1038/s41392-021-00631-2

Chirikos, T., & Nestel, G. (1985). Further Evidence on the Economic Effects of Poor Health. *The Review of Economics and Statistics, 67*(1), 61-69. doi:10.2307/1928435

Chu, J. (2017, January 19). *Study: Technological progress alone won't stem resource use.* MIT News. https://news.mit.edu/2017/technological-progress-alone-stem-consumption-materials-0119

Chung, C. L., Lawrence, I., Hoffman, M., Elgindi, D., Nadhan, K., Potnis, M., Jin, A., Sershon, C., Binnebose, R., Lorenzini, A., & Sell, C. (2019). Topical rapamycin reduces markers of senescence and aging in human skin: an exploratory, prospective, randomized trial. *GeroScience, 41*(6), 861–869. https://doi.org/10.1007/s11357-019-00113-y

Cohen B., & Menken J. (2006). Aging in Sub-Saharan Africa: Recommendation for Furthering Research. *National Academies Press (US).* 3-5. https://www.ncbi.nlm.nih.gov/books/NBK20296/

Colcombe, S. J., Kramer, A. F., Erickson, K. I., Scalf, P., McAuley, E., Cohen, N. J., Webb, A., Jerome, G. J., Marquez, D. X., & Elavsky, S. (2004). Cardiovascular fitness, cortical plasticity, and aging. *Proceedings of the National Academy of Sciences of the United States of America, 101*(9), 3316–3321. https://doi.org/10.1073/pnas.0400266101

Colicino, E., Marioni, R., Ward-Caviness, C., Gondalia, R., Guan, W., Chen, B., Tsai, P. C., Huan, T., Xu, G., Golareh, A., Schwartz, J., Vokonas, P., Just, A., Starr, J. M., McRae, A. F., Wray, N. R., Visscher, P. M., Bressler, J., Zhang, W., Tanaka, T., … Baccarelli, A. (2020). Blood DNA methylation sites predict death risk in a longitudinal study of 12, 300 individuals. *Aging, 12*(14), 14092–14124. https://doi.org/10.18632/aging.103408

Conger, C. (2008). *Could we clone our organs to be used in a transplant?* HowStuffWorks. https://science.howstuffworks.com/life/genetic/cloned-organ-transplant.htm

Cook, S. J., Jarrell, T. A., Brittin, C. A., Wang, Y., Bloniarz, A. E., Yakovlev, M. A., Nguyen, K., Tang, L. T., Bayer, E. A., Duerr, J. S., Bülow, H. E., Hobert, O., Hall, D. H., & Emmons, S. W. (2019). Whole-animal connectomes of both Caenorhabditis elegans sexes. *Nature, 571*(7763), 63–71. https://doi.org/10.1038/s41586-019-1352-7

De Gray, A. (2008). Combating the Tithonus Error: What Works? *Rejuvenation Research, 11*(4), 713-715. DOI:10.1089/rej.2008.0775

De Guia, R. M., Agerholm, M., Nielsen, T. S., Consitt, L. A., Søgaard, D., Helge, J. W., Larsen, S., Brandauer, J., Houmard, J. A., & Treebak, J. T. (2019). Aerobic and resistance exercise training reverses age-dependent decline in NAD+ salvage capacity in human skeletal muscle. Physiological reports, 7(12), e14139. https://doi.org/10.14814/phy2.14139

De Los Angeles, A., Pho, N., & Redmond, D. E., Jr (2018). Generating Human Organs via Interspecies Chimera Formation: Advances and Barriers. *The Yale journal of biology and medicine, 91*(3), 333–342.

De Unamuno, M. (1954). *The Tragic Sense of Life in Men and Nations* (J. E. C. Flitch, Trans.). Dover Publications, Inc. (Original work published 1912). Accessed through The Project Gutenberg. https://www.gutenberg.org/files/14636/14636-h/14636-h.htm

DeGrey, A. D. N. J., & Rae, M. (2007). *Ending aging: The rejuvenation breakthroughs that could reverse human aging in our lifetime.* New York: St. Martin's Press.

Di Daniele, N., Noce, A., Vidiri, M. F., Moriconi, E., Marrone, G., Annicchiarico-Petruzzelli, M., D'Urso, G., Tesauro, M., Rovella, V., & de Lorenzo, A. (2016). Impact of Mediterranean diet on metabolic syndrome, cancer and longevity. *Oncotarget, 8*(5), 8947–8979. https://doi.org/10.18632/oncotarget.13553

Di, Z., Liu, B., Zhao, J., Gu, Z., Zhao, Y., & Li, L. (2020). An orthogonally regulatable DNA nanodevice for spatiotemporally controlled biorecognition and tumor treatment. *Science advances, 6*(25), eaba9381. https://doi.org/10.1126/sciadv.aba9381

Douglas, S. M., Bachelet, I., & Church, G. M. (2012). A logic-gated nanorobot for targeted transport of molecular payloads. *Science (New York, N.Y.), 335*(6070), 831–834. https://doi.org/10.1126/science.1214081

Dumas, A., & Turner, B. S. (2015). Introduction: Human Longevity, Utopia, and Solidarity. *Sociological Quarterly, 56*(1), 1–17. https://doi.org/10.1111/tsq.12081

Editors of Encyclopaedia Britannica, The (2007, December 12). *Tithonus.* Encyclopaedia Britannica. https://www.britannica.com/topic/Tithonus-Greek-mythology

Editors of Encyclopaedia Britannica, The (2017, April 26). *Flying Dutchman.* Encyclopedia Britannica. https://www.britannica.com/topic/Flying-Dutchman

Editors of Encyclopaedia Britannica, The (2020, May 6). *Soul.* Encyclopedia Britannica. https://www.britannica.com/topic/soul-religion-and-philosophy

Editors of Encyclopaedia Britannica, The (2021, Mar 26). *Reincarnation.* Encyclopedia Britannica. https://www.britannica.com/topic/reincarnation

Ekerdt, D. J., Koss, C. S., Li, A., Münch, A., Lessenich, S., & Fung, H. H. (2017). Is longevity a value for older adults?. Journal of aging studies, 43, 46–52. https://doi.org/10.1016/j.jaging.2017.10.002

Erö, C., Gewaltig, M. O., Keller, D., & Markram, H. (2018). A Cell Atlas for the Mouse Brain. *Frontiers in neuroinformatics,* 12, 84. https://doi.org/10.3389/fninf.2018.00084

Ewen, H. H., Nikzad-Terhune, K., & Dassel, K. B. (2020). Exploring Beliefs about Agingand Faith: Development of the Judeo-Christian Religious Beliefs and Aging Scale. *Behavioural Sciences, 10*(9). https://doi.org/10.3390/bs10090139

Fahy, G. M., Brooke, R. T., Watson, J. P., Good, Z., Vasanawala, S. S., Maecker, H., Leipold, M. D., Lin, D., Kobor, M. S., & Horvath, S. (2019). Reversal of epigenetic aging and immunosenescent trends in humans. *Aging cell, 18*(6), e13028. https://doi.org/10.1111/acel.13028

Farmer, N. (2002). *The House of the Scorpion.* Atheneum Books.

Finch. C. (2010). Evolving Views of Ageing and Longevity from Homer to Hippocrates: Emergence of Natural PActors, Persistence of the Supernatural. *Greece & Rome, 57*(2), second series, 355-377. Retrieved July 17, 2021, from http://www.jstor.org/stable/40929484

Fontana, L., & Klein, S. (2007). Aging, adiposity, and calorie restriction. *JAMA, 297*(9), 986–994. https://doi.org/10.1001/jama.297.9.986

Fontana, L., Partridge, L., & Longo, V. D. (2010). Extending healthy life span--from yeast to humans. *Science (New York, N.Y.), 328*(5976), 321–326. https://doi.org/10.1126/science.1172539

Francese, C. (2018, February 24). Weighing Spartan Sacrifice. Dickinson Blogs. https://blogs.dickinson.edu/classicalstudies/tag/sparta/

Furman, D., Campisi, J., Verdin, E., Carrera-Bastos, P., Targ, S., Franceschi, C., Ferrucci, L., Gilroy, D. W., Fasano, A., Miller, G. W., Miller, A. H., Mantovani, A., Weyand, C. M., Barzilai, N., Goronzy, J. J., Rando, T. A., Effros, R. B., Lucia, A., Kleinstreuer, N., & Slavich, G. M. (2019). Chronic inflammation in the etiology of disease across the life span. *Nature medicine, 25*(12), 1822–1832. https://doi.org/10.1038/s41591-019-0675-0

Gatiss, M., Moffat, S., Venture, S., & Irving, B. (Executive Producers). (January 1 - January 3, 2020). *Dracula* [TV series]. Hartswood Films.

GBD 2016 Alcohol Collaborators (2018). Alcohol use and burden for 195 countries and territories, 1990-2016: a systematic analysis for the Global Burden of Disease Study 2016. *Lancet (London, England), 392*(10152), 1015–1035. https://doi.org/10.1016/S0140-6736(18)31310-2

Gems, D. (2011). Tragedy and delight: the ethics of decelerated ageing. *Philosophical Transactions of the Royal Society B, 366*(1561), 108-112. https://doi.org/10.1098/rstb.2010.0288

Globerman, S. (2021). *Canada's Aging Population and Income Support Programs.* Fraser Institute.

Globerman, S. (2021). *Canadian Seniors Will Consume 71.4 Percent of Total Health Care Expenditures in 2040.* Fraser Institute.

Gorman, A. G. (2016). Williams and the Desirability of Body-Bound Immortality Revisited. *European Journal of Philosophy, 25*(4), 1062-1083. https://doi.org/10.1111/ejop.12184

Gorry, D., Slavov, Sita., (2021). The effect of retirement on health biomarkers. Journal of Economics & Human Biology, Volume 40.

Grabowska, W., Sikora, E., & Bielak-Zmijewska, A. (2017). Sirtuins, a promising target in slowing down the ageing process. Biogerontology, 18(4), 447–476. https://doi.org/10.1007/s10522-017-9685-9

Hachmo, Y., Hadanny, A., Abu Hamed, R., Daniel-Kotovsky, M., Catalogna, M., Fishlev, G., Lang, E., Polak, N., Doenyas, K., Friedman, M., Zemel, Y., Bechor, Y., & Efrati, S. (2020). Hyperbaric oxygen therapy increases telomere length and decreases immunosenescence in isolated blood cells: a prospective trial. *Aging, 12*(22), 22445–22456. https://doi.org/10.18632/aging.202188

Hameroff, S., & Penrose, R. (2014). Consciousness in the universe: a review of the 'Orch OR' theory. *Physics of life reviews, 11*(1), 39–78. https://doi.org/10.1016/j.plrev.2013.08.002

Hasker, W., & Taliaferro, C. (2019, March 21). *Afterlife.* Stanford Encyclopedia of Philosophy. https://plato.stanford.edu/entries/afterlife/

Harrison, D. E., Strong, R., Alavez, S., Astle, C. M., DiGiovanni, J., Fernandez, E., Flurkey, K., Garratt, M., Gelfond, J., Javors, M. A., Levi, M., Lithgow, G. J., Macchiarini, F., Nelson, J. F., Sukoff Rizzo, S. J., Slaga, T. J., Stearns, T., Wilkinson, J. E., & Miller, R. A. (2019). Acarbose improves health and lifespan in aging HET3 mice. *Aging cell, 18*(2), e12898. https://doi.org/10.1111/acel.12898

Hauser, L. (n.d.) *Chinese Room Argument.* Internet Encyclopedia of Philosophy. https://iep.utm.edu/chineser/

Hayano, M. (2019). DNA Break-Induced Epigenetic Drift as a Cause of Mammalian Aging. *bioRxiv,* 808659. https://doi.org/10.1101/808659

Heidegger, M. (1978). Being and Time. Wiley-Blackwell. *Is immortality unethical?* (n.d.). DebateWise. https://debatewise.org/3102-is-immortality-unethical/

Hernaes, E., Markussen, S., Piggott, J., & Vestad, O. L. (2013). Does retirement age impact mortality? *Journal of health economics, 32*(3), 586-598.

Horvath, S., & Raj, K. (2018). DNA methylation-based biomarkers and the epigenetic clock theory of ageing. Nature reviews. *Genetics, 19*(6), 371–384. https://doi.org/10.1038/s41576-018-0004-3

Hubbard, T. J., & Denegar, C. R. (2004). Does Cryotherapy Improve Outcomes With Soft Tissue Injury?. *Journal of athletic training, 39*(3), 278–279.

Hummer, R. A., & Hernandez, E. M. (2013). The Effect of Educational Attainment on Adult Mortality in the United States. *Population bulletin, 68*(1), 1–16.

Imai, S. I., & Guarente, L. (2016). It takes two to tango: NAD+ and sirtuins in aging/longevity control. *NPJ aging and mechanisms of disease, 2,* 16017. https://doi.org/10.1038/npjamd.2016.17

Jaul, E., & Barron, J. (2017). Age-Related Diseases and Clinical and Public Health Implications for the 85 Years Old and Over Population. *Frontiers in public health, 5,* 335. https://doi.org/10.3389/fpubh.2017.00335

Kadowaki, H., Nishitoh, H., Urano, F., Sadamitsu, C., Matsuzawa, A., Takeda, K., Masutani, H., Yodoi, J., Urano, Y., Nagano, T., & Ichijo, H. (2005). Amyloid beta induces neuronal cell death through ROS-mediated ASK1 activation. *Cell death and differentiation, 12*(1), 19–24. https://doi.org/10.1038/sj.cdd.4401528

Kahn, A., & Olsen, A. (2009). Stress to the rescue: is hormesis a 'cure' for aging?. *Dose-response: a publication of International Hormesis Society, 8*(1), 48–52. https://doi.org/10.2203/dose-response.09-031.Olsen

Kang, S., Moser, V. A., Svendsen, C. N., & Goodridge, H. S. (2020). Rejuvenating the blood and bone marrow to slow aging-associated cognitive decline and Alzheimer's disease. *Communications biology, 3*(1), 69. https://doi.org/10.1038/s42003-020-0797-4

Karasawa, M., Curhan, K. B., Markus, H. R., Kitayama, S. S., Love, G. D., Radler, B. T., & Ryff, C. D. (2011). Cultural perspectives on aging and well-being: A comparison of Japan and the United States. *The International Journal of Aging and Human Development, 73*(1), 73-98.

Kaul, S., Gulati, N., Verma, D., Mukherjee, S., & Nagaich, U. (2018). Role of Nanotechnology in Cosmeceuticals: A Review of Recent Advances. *Journal of pharmaceutics, 2018*, 3420204. https://doi.org/10.1155/2018/3420204

Katz, S. (2001/2002) Growing Older without Aging? Positive Aging, Anti-ageism, and Anti-aging, Generations 25: 27.

Kikuchi, S., Shinpo, K., Takeuchi, M., Yamagishi, S., Makita, Z., Sasaki, N., & Tashiro, K. (2003). Glycation--a sweet tempter for neuronal death. Brain research. *Brain research reviews, 41*(2-3), 306–323. https://doi.org/10.1016/s0165-0173(02)00273-4

Kirkland, J. L., & Tchkonia, T. (2020). Senolytic drugs: from discovery to translation. *Journal of internal medicine, 288*(5), 518–536. https://doi.org/10.1111/joim.13141

Kulkarni, A. S., Gubbi, S., & Barzilai, N. (2020). Benefits of Metformin in Attenuating the Hallmarks of Aging. *Cell metabolism, 32*(1), 15–30. https://doi.org/10.1016/j.cmet.2020.04.001

Kurzweil, R. (1993). *The Age of Spiritual Machines: When Computers Exceed Human Intelligence.* Viking Press

Lang, F. R., & Rupprecht, F. S. (2019). Motivation for Longevity Across the Life Span: An Emerging Issue. *Innovation in Aging, 3*(2). https://doi.org/10.1093/geroni/igz014

Lee, B. P., Smith, M., Buffenstein, R., & Harries, L. W. (2020). Negligible senescence in naked mole rats may be a consequence of well-maintained splicing regulation. *GeroScience, 42,* 633-651. https://doi.org/10.1007/s11357-019-00150-7

Li, S., Jiang, Q., Liu, S., Zhang, Y., Tian, Y., Song, C., Wang, J.,... Zhao, Y. (2018). A DNA nanorobot functions as a cancer therapeutic in response to a molecular trigger in vivo. *Nature biotechnology, 36*(3), 258–264. https://doi.org/10.1038/nbt.4071

Lithgow, G. J., White, T. M., Melov, S., & Johnson, T. E. (1995). Thermotolerance and extended life-span conferred by single-gene mutations and induced by thermal stress. *Proceedings of the National Academy of Sciences of the United States of America, 92*(16), 7540–7544. https://doi.org/10.1073/pnas.92.16.7540

Liu, J. (2013, August 6). Living to 120 and Beyond: Americans' Views on Aging, Medical Advances and Radical Life Extension. Pew Research Center's Religion & Public Life Project. https://www.pewforum.org/2013/08/06/living-to-120-and-beyond-americans-views-on-aging-medical-advances-and-radical-life-extension/

Löckenhoff, C. E., De Fruyt, F., Terracciano, A., McCrae, R. R., De Bolle, M., Costa, P. T., Jr, Aguilar-Vafaie, M. E., Ahn, C. K., Ahn, H. N., Alcalay, L., Allik, J., Avdeyeva, T. V., Barbaranelli, C., Benet-Martinez, V., Blatný, M., Bratko, D., Cain, T. R., Crawford, J. T., Lima, M. P., Ficková, E., ... Yik, M. (2009). Perceptions of aging across 26 cultures and their culture-level associates. *Psychology and aging, 24*(4), 941–954. https://doi.org/10.1037/a0016901

Longo, V.D., Di Tano, M., Mattson, M.P. *et al.* Intermittent and periodic fasting, longevity and disease. *Nat Aging* 1, 47–59 (2021). https://doi.org/10.1038/s43587-020-00013-3

Loos E., Ivan L. (2018) Visual Ageism in the Media. In: Ayalon L., Tesch-Römer C. (eds) Contemporary Perspectives on Ageism. International Perspectives on Aging, vol 19. Springer, Cham. https://doi.org/10.1007/978-3-319-73820-8_11

López-Otín, C., Blasco, M. A., Partridge, L., Serrano, M., & Kroemer, G. (2013). The hallmarks of aging. *Cell, 153*(6), 1194–1217. https://doi.org/10.1016/j.cell.2013.05.039

Lorenz, H. (2009, June 21). *Ancient Theories of Soul.* Stanford Encyclopedia of Philosophy.https://plato.stanford.edu/entries/ancient-soul/

Lu, Y., Brommer, B., Tian, X., Krishnan, A., Meer, M., Wang, C., Vera, D. L., Zeng, Q., Yu, D., Bonkowski, M. S., Yang, J. H., Zhou, S., Hoffmann, E. M., Karg, M. M., Schultz, M. B., Kane, A. E., Davidsohn, N., Korobkina, E., Chwalek, K., Rajman, L. A., ... Sinclair, D. A. (2020). Reprogramming to recover youthful epigenetic information and restore vision. *Nature, 588*(7836), 124–129. https://doi.org/10.1038/s41586-020-2975-4

Lucas, T., Horton, R. (2019). The 21st-century great food transformation. *The Lancet, 393*(10170), 386-387. https://doi.org/10.1016/S0140-6736(18)33179-9

Lynch, F. (2016). America's Road to "Post Familialism. *Society, 53*(2), 211–217. https://doi-org.login.ezproxy.library.ualberta.ca/10.1007/s12115-016-9997-4

MacDonald, B.-J., & Hirdes, J. (2019). *The Future Co$t of Long-Term Care in Canada.* Fraser Institute.

Mackey, T. (2003). An ethical assessment of anti-aging medicine. *Journal of Anti-Aging Medicine, 6*(3), 187-204. https://doi.org/10.1089/109454503322733045

Mahla R. S. (2016). Stem Cells Applications in Regenerative Medicine and Disease Therapeutics. *International journal of cell biology, 2016,* 6940283. https://doi.org/10.1155/2016/6940283

Malchesky, P. S., Murray, K. D., Olsen, D. B., & Schoen, F. J. (1996). Artificial Organs.

Mark, J. J. (2021, May 15). The Eternal Life of Gilgamesh. World History Encyclopedia. https://www.worldhistory.org/article/192/the-eternal-life-of-gilgamesh/.

Markus, M. A., & Morris, B. J. (2008). Resveratrol in prevention and treatment of common clinical conditions of aging. *Clinical interventions in aging, 3*(2), 331–339.

Matsukura, R., Shimizutani, S., Mitsuyama, N., Lee, S., Ogawa, N., 2018. Untapped work capacity among old persons and their potential contributions to the "silver dividend" in Japan. J. Econ. *Ageing 12,* 236–249. https://doi.org/10.1016/j.jeoa.2017.01.002.

Minkel, J. R. (2008, March 4). "Methuselah" Mutation Linked to Longer Life. Scientific American. https://www.scientificamerican.com/article/methuselah-mutation-linked-to-long-life/.

Mitchell S.(2004). Gilgamesh : A New English Version. New York :Free Press

Mkrtchyan, G. V., Abdelmohsen, K., Andreux, P., Bagdonaite, I., Barzilai, N., Brunak, S., Cabreiro, F., de Cabo, R., Campisi, J., Cuervo, A. M., Demaria, M., Ewald, C. Y., Fang, E. F., Faragher, R., Ferrucci, L., Freund, A., Silva-García, C. G., Georgievskaya, A., Gladyshev, V. N., Glass, D. J., … Scheibye-Knudsen, M. (2020). ARDD 2020: from aging mechanisms to interventions. *Aging, 12*(24), 24484–24503. https://doi.org/10.18632/aging.202454

Mokhtare, M., Valizadeh, S. M., & Emadian, O. (2013). Lower Gastrointestinal Bleeding due to Non-Steroid Anti-Inflammatory Drug-Induced Colopathy Case Report and Literature Review. *Middle East journal of digestive diseases, 5*(2), 107–111.

Moravec, H. (1999). *Robot: Mere Machine to Transcendent Mind.* Oxford University Press.

Murphy, K. M. & Topel, R. H. The value of health and longevity. *J. Polit. Econ. 114*, 871–904.https://doi.org/10.1086/508033(2006).

Murthy S. K. (2007). Nanoparticles in modern medicine: state of the art and future challenges. *International journal of nanomedicine, 2*(2), 129–141.

New Living Translation Bible. (2015). Bible Gateway. https://www.biblegateway.com/

Nenna, A., Nappi, F., Avtaar Singh, S. S., Sutherland, F. W., Di Domenico, F., Chello, M., & Spadaccio, C. (2015). Pharmacologic Approaches Against Advanced Glycation End Products (AGEs) in Diabetic Cardiovascular Disease. *Research in cardiovascular medicine, 4*(2), e26949. https://doi.org/10.5812/cardiovascmed.4(2)2015.26949

Neuralink. (2020, August 28). Neuralink Progress Update, Summer 2020. YouTube.

Neuralink. (n.d.). *Engineering with the Brain.* Retrieved from Neuralink: https://neuralink.com/applications/

Newman A. & Murabito J. M. (2013) The Epidemiology of Longevity and Exceptional Survival, Epidemiologic Reviews, Volume 35, Issue 1, 2013, Pages 181–197, https://doi.org/10.1093/epirev/mxs013

Ocampo, A., Reddy, P., Martinez-Redondo, P., Platero-Luengo, A., Hatanaka, F., Hishida, T., Li, M.,… Izpisua Belmonte, J. C. (2016). In Vivo Amelioration of Age-Associated Hallmarks by Partial Reprogramming. *Cell, 167*(7), 1719–1733.e12. https://doi.org/10.1016/j.cell.2016.11.052

Pallardy, R. (2020). Elizabeth Báthory. Encyclopedia Britannica. https://www.britannica.com/biography/Elizabeth-Bathory

Panas, M., Poulakou-Rebelakou, E., Kalfakis, N., & Vassilopoulos, D. (2012). The Byzantine Empress Zoe Porphyrogenita and the quest for eternal youth. *Journal of Cosmetic Dermatology, 11*(3), 245–248. https://doi.org/10.1111/j.1473-2165.2012.00629.x

Pandika M. (2019). Looking to Young Blood to Treat the Diseases of Aging. *ACS central science, 5*(9), 1481–1484. https://doi.org/10.1021/acscentsci.9b00902

Papanicolas, I., Marino, A., Lorenzoni, L., & Jha, A. (2020). Comparison of Health Care Spending by Age in 8 High-Income Countries. *JAMA network open, 3*(8), e2014688. https://doi.org/10.1001/jamanetworkopen.2020.14688

Patrick, S. (2019). *FoundMyFitness Topic - Sauna.* FoundMyFitness. https://www.foundmyfitness.com/topics/sauna

Patrick, S. (2016). *FoundMyFitness Topic - How Cryotherapy Affects the Brain, the Immune System, Metabolism, and Athletic Performance.* FoundMyFitness. https://www.foundmyfitness.com/episodes/cold-stress-hormesis

Pereira, F. (2020, January 23). *Is Immortality Desirable?.* 1000 Word Philosophy. https://1000wordphilosophy.com/2020/01/23/is-immortality-desirable/#_ftn23

Perrault, R., Shoham, Y., Brynjolfsson, E., Clark, J., Etchemendy, J., Grosz, B., Niebles, J. (2019). *The AI Index 2019 Annual Report.* Stanford University

Petersen, A. (2015) Hope in Health: The Socio-politics of Optimism. Basingstoke: Palgrave Macmillan.

Petersen, A. Capitalising on ageing anxieties: Promissory discourse and the creation of an 'anti-ageing treatment' market. *Journal of Sociology. 2018;54*(2):191-202 doi:10.1177/1440783318766165

Petralia, R. S., Mattson, M. P., & Yao, P. J. (2014). Aging and longevity in the simplest animals and the quest for immortality. *Ageing research reviews, 16,* 66–82. https://doi.org/10.1016/j.arr.2014.05.003

Pijnenburg, A. M., & Leget, C. (2007). Who wants to live forever? Three arguments against extending the human lifespan. *Journal of Medical Ethics, 33*(10), 585-587. http://dx.doi.org/10.1136/jme.2006.017822.

Pletcher, S. D. (2002). Mitigating the Tithonus Error: Genetic Analysis of Mortality Phenotypes. *SAGE KE, 2002*(37), 14. DOI: 10.1126/sageke.2002.37.pe14

Post, S. G. (2004). Anti-Aging Medicine: The History: Establishing an Appropriate Ethical Framework: The Moral Conversation Around the Goal of Prolongevity. *The Journals of Gerontology: Series A, 59*(6), B534–B539. https://doi.org/10.1093/gerona/59.6.B534

Post, S. G., & Binstock, R. H. (2004). *The fountain of youth cultural, scientific, and ethical perspectives on a biomedical goal.* Oxford University Press.

Pushkin, A., & Lermontov, M. (1983). The Demon. In *Narrative Poems by Alexander Pushkin and by Mikhail Lermontov* (Johnston, C., Trans.) (pp. 107-144). (Original work published 1841). Accessed through http://faculty.washington.edu/jdwest/russ430/demon.pdf

Rajpathak, S. N., Liu, Y., Ben-David, O., Reddy, S., Atzmon, G., Crandall, J., & Barzilai, N. (2011). Lifestyle factors of people with exceptional longevity. *Journal of the American Geriatrics Society, 59*(8), 1509–1512. https://doi.org/10.1111/j.1532-5415.2011.03498.x

Ramezani, H., & Dietz, H. (2020). Building machines with DNA molecules. Nature reviews. *Genetics, 21*(1), 5–26. https://doi.org/10.1038/s41576-019-0175-6

Ratner, A. S. Hoffman, F. J. Schoen, & J. E. Lemons (Eds.) *Biomaterials Science: An Introduction to Materials in Medicine* (pp. 389-412). Academic Press. https://doi.org/10.1016/C2009-0-20916-0

Redman, L. M., & Ravussin, E. (2011). Caloric restriction in humans: impact on physiological, psychological, and behavioral outcomes. *Antioxidants & redox signaling, 14*(2), 275–287. https://doi.org/10.1089/ars.2010.3253

Reimann, M. W., Gevaert, M., Shi, Y., Lu, H., Markram, H., & Muller, E. (2019). A null model of the mouse whole-neocortex micro-connectome. *Nature communications, 10*(1), 3903. https://doi.org/10.1038/s41467-019-11630-x

Reincarnation (2019, July 27). New World Encyclopedia. https://www.newworldencyclopedia.org/entry/reincarnation

Resources and Consumption (n.d.). Population Matters. https://populationmatters.org/resources-consumption

Rice, D. P., & Fineman, N. (2004). Economic implications of increased longevity in the United States. Annu. Rev. Public Health, 25, 457-473.

Rohland, L. (2020). Fountain of Youth. Salem Press Encyclopedia.

Rogers, C. T. (2020, April 9). *Dracula's Biggest Enemy — Part II.* Medium. https://medium.com/the-philosophers-stone/draculas-biggest-enemy-part-ii-9c5b3ecd4ef5

Rosemary Blieszner, & Victoria Hilkevitch Bedford. (2012). Handbook of Families and Aging, 2nd Edition: Vol. 2nd ed. Praeger.

Roser, M., Ortiz-Ospina, E., Ritchie, H. (2013). "Life Expectancy". OurWorldInData.org. https://ourworldindata.org/life-expectancy

Sagar, P. (2018). *There's a big problem with immortality: it goes on and on.* Aeon. https://aeon.co/essays/theres-a-big-problem-with-immortality-it-goes-on-and-on

Salleh M. R. (2008). Life event, stress and illness. *The Malaysian journal of medical sciences : MJMS, 15*(4), 9–18.

Sandberg A. (2013) Feasibility of Whole Brain Emulation. In: Müller V. (eds) Philosophy and Theory of Artificial Intelligence. Studies in Applied Philosophy, Epistemology and Rational Ethics, vol 5. Springer, Berlin, Heidelberg. https://doi.org/10.1007/978-3-642-31674-6_19

Sandeep, S. (2018, June 6-7). *"Magical Organ": Cloning of organ to be used in a Transplant* [Conference Session]. 24th International Conference on Cardiovascular and Thoracic Surgery, Osaka, Japan.https://www.longdom.org/proceedings/magical-organ-cloning-of-organ-to-be-used-in-a-transplant-57305.html#

Serling, R. (Writer), Venable, L. (Writer), & Brahm, J. (Director). (1959, November 20). Time Enough at Last (Season 1, Episode 8) [TV series episode]. In Serling, R. (Executive Producer), *The Twilight Zone.* Cayuga Productions; CBS Productions.

Shelly, M. (1833). *The Mortal Immortal.*

Sinclair, D. A., LaPlante, M. D., & Delphia, C. (2019). *Lifespan: Why we age--and why we don't have to.*

Skylar-Scott, M. A., Uzel, S., Nam, L. L., Ahrens, J. H., Truby, R. L., Damaraju, S., & Lewis, J. A. (2019). Biomanufacturing of organ-specific tissues with high cellular density and embedded vascular channels. *Science advances,* 5(9), eaaw2459. https://doi.org/10.1126/sciadv.aaw2459

Snyder, Z. (Director). (2007). *300* [Film]. Legendary Pictures; Virtual Studios; Atmospheric Entertainment MM; Hollywood Gang Productions.

Spielberg, S. (Director). (1989). *Indiana Jones and the Last Crusade [Film].* Lucasfilm Ltd.

Strong, K., Mathers, C., Leeder, S., & Beaglehole, R. (2005). Preventing chronic diseases: how many lives can we save?. *Lancet (London, England), 366*(9496), 1578–1582. https://doi.org/10.1016/S0140-6736(05)67341-2

Swift, J. (1726). *Gulliver's Travels.* Benjamin Motte.

Tabatabaie, V., Atzmon, G., Rajpathak, S. N., Freeman, R., Barzilai, N., & Crandall, J. (2011). Exceptional longevity is associated with decreased reproduction. *Aging, 3*(12), 1202–1205. https://doi.org/10.18632/aging.100415

Tanuseputro, P., Wodchis, W. P., Fowler, R., Walker, P., Bai, Y. Q., Bronskill, S. E., & Manuel, D. (2015). The health care cost of dying: a population-based retrospective cohort study of the last year of life in Ontario, Canada. *PloS one, 10*(3), e0121759. https://doi.org/10.1371/journal.pone.0121759

Than, K. (2006, May 23). *The Ethical Dilemmas of Immortality.* Live Science. https://www.livescience.com/10465-ethical-dilemmas-immortality.html

__Thayer, C., & Skufca, L. (2019)__. Media Image Landscape: Age Representation in Online Images. AARP. Published. https://doi.org/10.26419/res.00339.001

Timmermans, S. (2017) Anti-ageing, advertising feature. The Age, 23 February: 28.

Timmermans, S. and M. Berg (2003) The Gold Standard: The Challenge of Evidence-based Medicine and Standardization in Healthcare. Philadelphia, PA: Temple University Press.

Traulsen, A., & Mehnert, K. (2019, June 12). *Those who live longer have fewer children.* Max-Planck-Gesellschaft. https://www.mpg.de/13559984/those-who-live-longer-have-fewer-children

United Nations. "World Population Prospects 2019, Population Data, File: Population Growth Rate, Medium Variant Fertility tab". United Nations Population Division.

University of California - Berkeley. (2020, June 15). Diluting blood plasma

Uribarri, J., Woodruff, S., Goodman, S., Cai, W., Chen, X., Pyzik, R., Yong, A., Striker, G. E., & Vlassara, H. (2010). Advanced glycation end products in foods and a practical guide to their reduction in the diet. *Journal of the American Dietetic Association, 110*(6), 911–16.e12. https://doi.org/10.1016/j.jada.2010.03.018

Vasto, S., Buscemi, S., Barera, A., di Carlo, M., Accardi, G., & Caruso, C. (2014). Mediterranean Diet and Healthy Ageing: A Sicilian Perspective. *Gerontology, 60*(6), 508–518. https://doi.org/10.1159/000363060

Vincent, J. (2013). The anti-aging movement. In Ethics, health policy and (anti-) aging: Mixed blessings (pp. 29-40). Springer, Dordrecht.

Vollset, S. E., Goren, E., Yuan, C. W., Cao, J., Smith, A. E., Hsiao, T., Bisignano, C., Azhar, G. S., Castro, E., Chalek, J., Dolgert, A. J., Frank, T., Fukutaki, K., Hay, S. I., Lozano, R., Mokdad, A. H., Nandakumar, V., Pierce, M., Pletcher, M., Robalik, T., ... Murray, C. (2020). Fertility, mortality, migration, and population scenarios for 195 countries and territories from 2017 to 2100: a forecasting analysis for the Global Burden of Disease Study. *Lancet (London, England), 396*(10258), 1285–1306. https://doi.org/10.1016/S0140-6736(20)30677-2

Waldo, D., and Lazenby, H. 1984. Demographic characteristics and health care use and expenditures by the aged in the U.S.: 1977–1984. *Health Care Financing Review* 6(1):1–29.

Wang, W., Zheng, Y., Sun, S., Li, W., Song, M., Ji, Q., Wu, Z., Liu, Z., Fan, Y., Liu, F., Li, J., Esteban, C. R., Wang, S., Zhou, Q., Belmonte, J., Zhang, W., Qu, J., Tang, F., & Liu, G. H. (2021). A genome-wide CRISPR-based screen identifies KAT7 as a driver of cellular senescence. *Science translational medicine, 13*(575), eabd2655. https://doi.org/10.1126/scitranslmed.abd2655

Weinberg, B. A., & Galenson, D. W. (2005). Creative careers: The life cycles of Nobel laureates in economics (No. 11799). National Bureau of Economic Research.

Weitzmann, M. N., Ha, S. W., Vikulina, T., Roser-Page, S., Lee, J. K., & Beck, G. R., Jr (2015). Bioactive silica nanoparticles reverse age-associated bone loss in mice. *Nanomedicine : nanotechnology, biology, and medicine, 11*(4), 959–967. https://doi.org/10.1016/j.nano.2015.01.013

Weon, B. M., & Je, J. H. (2009). Theoretical estimation of maximum human lifespan. *Biogerontology, 10*(1), 65–71. https://doi.org/10.1007/s10522-008-9156-4

Werner, C. M., Hecksteden, A., Morsch, A., Zundler, J., Wegmann, M., Kratzsch, J., Thiery, J., Hohl, M., Bittenbring, J. T., Neumann, F., Böhm, M., Meyer, T., & Laufs, U. (2019). Differential effects of endurance, interval, and resistance training on telomerase activity and telomere length in a randomized, controlled study. *European heart journal, 40*(1), 34–46. https://doi.org/10.1093/eurheartj/ehy585

Williams, G. C. (1999). The Tithonus Error in Modern Gerontology. *The Quarterly Review of Biology, 74*(4), 405-415. http://www.jstor.org/stable/2664720

Woo, J., Archard, D., Au, D., Bergstresser, S., Erler, A., Kwow, T., Newman, J., Tong, R., & Walker, T. (2019). Ethical perspectives on advances in biogerontology. *Aging Medicine, 2*(2), 99-103. https://doi.org/10.1002/agm2.12061

World Health Organization. (2020, December 9). *The top 10 causes of death.* Retrieved from who.int: https://www.who.int/news-room/fact-sheets/detail/the-top-10-causes-of-death

Worldometer (n.d.). Retrieved July 12 2021 from https://www.worldometers.info/

Xu, M., Pirtskhalava, T., Farr, J. N., Weigand, B. M., Palmer, A. K., Weivoda, M. M., Inman, C. L., Ogrodnik, M. B., Hachfeld, C. M., Fraser, D. G., Onken, J. L., Johnson, K. O., Verzosa, G. C., Langhi, L., Weigl, M., Giorgadze, N., LeBrasseur, N. K., Miller, J. D., Jurk, D., Singh, R. J., ... Kirkland, J. L. (2018). Senolytics improve physical function and increase lifespan in old age. *Nature medicine, 24*(8), 1246–1256. https://doi.org/10.1038/s41591-018-0092-9

Yoshino, J., Baur, J. A., & Imai, S. I. (2018). NAD+ Intermediates: The Biology and Therapeutic Potential of NMN and NR. *Cell metabolism, 27*(3), 513–528. https://doi.org/10.1016/j.cmet.2017.11.002

Zhang, Z. D., Milman, S., Lin, J. R., Wierbowski, S., Yu, H., Barzilai, N., Gorbunova, V., Ladiges, W. C., Niedernhofer, L. J., Suh, Y., Robbins, P. D., & Vijg, J. (2020). Genetics of extreme human longevity to guide drug discovery for healthy ageing. *Nature metabolism, 2*(8), 663–672. https://doi.org/10.1038/s42255-020-0247-0

Zitter, J. (2017, April 10). *Pricey Technology Is Keeping People Alive Who Don't Want to Live.* Wired. https://www.wired.com/2017/04/pricey-technology-keeping-people-alive-dont-want-live/

About The Authors

Thomas Banks, Madeline Langier, Rob Mcweeny, & Jonathan Wiebe are young students and professionals passionate about sharing information or knowledge.

Austin Mardon is an author, mental health advocate and assistant adjunct professor at the University of Alberta. He founded the Antarctic Institute of Canada and is married to Catherine Mardon. Together, the couple have written several books and remain community leaders in his hometown of Edmonton, Alberta.

Catherine Mardon is an author and social activist, having received multiple Bachelors, a Juris Doctor, and a Master's degree in a number of scientific, artistic, and theological fields. She is married to Austin Mardon and they have written several books together. They live in Austin's hometown of Edmonton, Alberta.

www.ingramcontent.com/pod-product-compliance
Lightning Source LLC
Chambersburg PA
CBHW050110170426
43198CB00014B/2523